cause a disturbance

If you can slice a melon or make a right-hand turn,
you can be a breakthrough innovator

cause a disturbance

If you can slice a melon or make a right-hand turn,
you can be a breakthrough innovator

by
Ken Tencer
and
John Paulo Cardoso

NEW YORK

Cause a Disturbance

© 2014 Spyder Works Inc.

Information on how to obtain copies of this book is available at www.causeadisturbance.com

Published in New York, New York, by Morgan James Publishing. Morgan James and The Entrepreneurial Publisher are trademarks of Morgan James, LLC. www.MorganJamesPublishing.com

The Morgan James Speakers Group can bring authors to your live event. For more information or to book an event visit The Morgan James Speakers Group at www.TheMorganJamesSpeakersGroup.com

FREE eBook edition for your existing eReader with purchase

PRINT NAME ABOVE

For more information, instructions, restrictions, and to register your copy, go to **www.bitlit.ca/readers/register** or use your QR Reader to scan the barcode:

ISBN 9781614489924 paperback
ISBN 9781614489931 eBook
ISBN 9781614489948 audio
ISBN 9781614489955 hardcover
Library of Congress Control Number: 2013951453

Cover Design by:
Spyder Works Inc.
www.spyderworksdesign.com

Interior Design by:
Tibor Choleva
www.blueappleworks.com

In an effort to support local communities, raise awareness and funds, Morgan James Publishing donates a percentage of all book sales for the life of each book to Habitat for Humanity Peninsula and Greater Williamsburg.

Get involved today, visit
www.MorganJamesBuilds.com

Habitat for Humanity®
Peninsula and Greater Williamsburg
Building Partner

"Adopt a Growth Mind-set: If you're always thinking about possibility, you'll find it. You'll keep creating the future."

– Sir Ken Robinson, *Fast Company* September 2013

Table of Contents

Preface

By Rick Spence

*President, Canadian Entrepreneur
Communications, National Entrepreneurship
Columnist,* National Post, *Former editor and
publisher,* PROFIT Magazine

So much has been written on innovation – why another book?

Because the need for businesses to add more value in everything they make and do, continues to intensify. Products are copyable, service is a commodity; only by constantly creating more value for customers (or for itself, through process innovation) can your business secure its future and enjoy profitable, sustainable growth.

Innovation is the practice of creating more value. There are lots of books, studies, blogs and websites that overcomplicate the concept of innovation, but only Ken Tencer and John Paulo Cardoso emphasize its simplicity. As *Cause A Disturbance* demonstrates again and again, you don't need a PhD or a team of white-coated scientists to create more innovative products and services. All you need, it turns out, is ongoing curiosity about how you can do things better, or cheaper, and a deep affinity for your customers that allows you to constantly devise new, better ways of meeting their wants and needs.

Anyone can do it. The message of this book is that anyone can rock their industry through successful innovation, regardless of the size of their business or the industry they're in. New products, complementary services and better processes are never more than an idea away. And the best of these ideas are low-risk and easy to pull off, because they usually involve doing things you are already doing – just doing them a little better, a little smarter, with a little more flair, intent or customer insight.

And yes, anyone can create a disturbance. When you perceive innovation as a sequence of safe, small steps into adjacent products, markets and ready-made opportunities, you realize there is no limit on your ability to innovate. Musical notation uses just a handful of notes, lines and symbols, with which composers have create infinite numbers of songs, symphonies and soundtracks; similarly, the tools of innovation are so inexpensive and powerful that they too can be mixed and mingled to create infinite numbers of plans, programs and opportunities. With the right attitude, anyone can create a stream of innovations that reduce costs, improve product quality, delight your customers and create loyal new ones.

Sounds too good to be true? Well, there is a catch. You have to train yourself to recognize where innovation opportunities may be lurking, and to ask yourself the right questions that stimulate new ideas. But no one makes it easier than Tencer and Cardoso. By condensing their simple, common-sense formula into this short, compelling and highly readable book, they have put innovation in the hands of any business person who truly wants to succeed.

If you can slice a melon or make a right-hand turn - or put a piece of cake on a stick - you too can be an innovator. That's the theme of this book, and it's never been so timely. Because fewer and fewer businesses today can get away with not innovating. Unless you're constantly offering new ways to improve your customer offerings or to compel your customers to come back more often, you are a sitting duck for any other entrepreneur who happens along and decides they want a piece of your action.

Cause A Disturbance is about disrupting your marketplace before someone else does. The title of this book may put some people off - it sounds so, well, disturbing. But in an age when rapid globalization and the still-growing power of the Internet are creating competitive challenges in every industry (whoever thought that Google would destroy newspapers, or that Amazon.com would challenge Wal-Mart's status as the world's largest retailer?), creating a disturbance is your best strategy for success. If you're standing still in your market, competitors know exactly where and how to take business away from you. If you're moving fast, constantly creating new stakeholder relationships and greater customer goodwill, competitors may still shoot at you - but they're going to miss. *Cause A Disturbance* could be the new mantra of business. For successful businesses, it will certainly become the new normal.

In this book, the strategists of Spyder Works draw on their skills and years of client experience to create a step-by-step guide to managing strategic innovation and diversification. I believe their dynamic but doable approach can revolutionize business by taking the pain, uncertainty and risk out of organic growth and expansion. Drawing on examples from their own business, from clients, and from global market leaders such as G Adventures and Coca-Cola (as well as lesser-known innovators such as OMI Industries and Weddingstar), they have synthesized successful growth strategies into a series of practical exercises that will help businesses understand their strengths, tell good opportunities from bad, and leap boldly (but never rashly) into new markets.

As a communications specialist, I am drawn especially to the Ken and John's insistence that companies need to understand who they are and what they do best before moving into new products and markets. In my experience, few organizations really understand their core competencies – the unique combination of assets, intelligence, track record and talent that constitute their competitive advantage. If you don't know what you do best, how can you possibly decide what to do next?

As Ken and John say, it's about evolution, not revolution.

In this book, your authors clearly explain what entrepreneurial thinking means. Know what you're good at. Learn how to communicate that strategic message, clearly and consistently, to make sure everyone on the team understands where they're going. Build strong, intimate relationships with your customers; know their needs as well as you do your own. Cultivate innovative thinking that emphasizes how you can do things better, or satisfy your customers' needs more completely – now and in the future. Map and compare competing opportunities, and then reinvent your business to serve the most promising *contiguous* niches. Involve your key team members throughout this process, and create metrics that will engage them and make sure the work gets done. The advice in this book outlines a series of "best practices" that can't help but result in a smarter, more focused, customer-facing organization.

Cause A Disturbance! Subscribe now to the notion that your business has to surprise and reward its customers more often. Look for adjacent opportunities to create more value and serve them better. Develop a company culture that values change over status quo, that dares to experiment, that learns from its failures and celebrates its victories. Imagine a business world where every market change is an opportunity, not a problem, and every client with a new pain comes to you for help first - because your company understands better than anyone else in the market that innovation, growth and success all come from meeting the customer's changing needs.

Fast-moving markets can be white-knuckle roller-coaster rides. But in my experience, the people who accept that their business is now in constant motion do better, have more fun – and attract a higher class of customers, employees and associates – than those who try to hold on to the past. Invest in tomorrow, not yesterday.

Anyone can be successful in business. But to sustain that success requires more than luck or a single good idea. It takes a disciplined, proven approach to creating results over time. You hold such an approach in your hands. Success is *this* close! Now go out and create a commotion. Delight your customers and confound your competitors. *Cause A Disturbance!*

Rick Spence

One

Simplifying Innovation

*If you can slice a melon or make a right-hand turn,
you can be a breakthrough innovator*

Chapter **1**

Innovation: Ouff!
That Sounds Difficult

Innovation isn't buried in your screensaver.
But if you tilt your head up, just a little bit, there's
a world of opportunity right in front of you.

Ken Tencer

Many people think that innovation is masked in complexity. In reality, successful innovation harnesses the obvious.

Take the cake pop for example. These deceptively simple desserts – frosted balls of cake on a lollipop stick – reflect everything that is inherently true about innovation. Created by baker/blogger Angie "Bakerella" Dudley in early 2008, they became an overnight sensation a month later when Martha Stewart invited Dudley to make cake pops on her TV show.

Cake pops were a simple but ingenious new use of a traditional product – an essential aspect of innovation. Their debut opened up huge opportunities for new sales and different creative offerings of the same basic product: batter and frosting on a stick. Why have cake pops been such a success? The concept reflected the world around us – a shift to healthier

Many people think that innovation is masked in complexity. In reality, successful innovation harnesses the obvious.

It's about surprising and delighting your customers and solving their problems.

lifestyles (or at least smaller portions), more frugal indulgences, and ease of access for people on the go – "Look ma, no fork!" It also met another criterion, bringing originality and a sense of fun to the baking and catering industries.

Covered with sprinkles or styled to resemble cupcakes, mini ice-cream cones, flowers, and even Christmas trees, cake pops are now popping up all over: at birthday parties (less messy than slices of cake), weddings, corporate events and family dinners – any place where gracious hosts and hostesses are competing to serve up "new," "unique" and "fun."

Understanding consumer needs and capitalizing on market shifts is the essence of innovation. It's continually re-engaging your customers by meeting their changing wants and needs, even anticipating new needs and meeting them before customers realize they exist. It's about surprising and delighting your customers and solving their problems. Do it. And watch your sales pop.

You can close more business in two months by becoming interested in other people than you can in two years by trying to get people interested in you.

Dale Carnegie

In the age of social media, customer relationships and brand loyalty have never been more important. It's all about relationships. Your ability to innovate is a core ingredient in not only building relationships with customers but also in keeping those relationships fresh and growing. Like marriages, partnerships and other human bonds, customer relationships require constant nurturing: through new and interesting ideas, new experiences, continual reaffirmation and frequent renewal. Relationships that aren't renewed and reinforced grow old and stale, and get discarded. It's that simple. If you want to build your brand and retain your customers – not to mention attract new ones – then innovation must be a part of your business equation.

INNOVATION + BRANDING = CUSTOMER RETENTION

Ironically, I enjoyed my first cake pop at Starbucks. Yes, that innovative global, social retail phenomenon built on nothing more than a cup of coffee. Actually, Starbucks was not founded just on a cup of coffee, but on the role that coffee plays in the human need for social interaction. We are still social animals, not just long distance online finger-typers. And funnily enough, while delighting in my first cake pop, I sipped a "Steamed Apple Juice" – more innovative product diversity at a coffee shop (one of the world's oldest retail concepts).

> *In the field of observation, chance favors the prepared mind.*
>
> Louis Pasteur (1822-1895)

During a presentation on product innovation in New York City, I was asked a great question: "What tools do I need to be an innovator?" My answer was simple and for many, surprising: "Your eyes and ears." Opportunities are all around us. When we take the time to notice them, they can stimulate more creative thoughts within each of us. And I really should have added "feet," because the day before I had walked 40 Manhattan blocks looking for interesting and outrageous inputs to spur my own innovative thinking. Here are two examples of what I found.

First, I noted that Ben & Jerry's had introduced a new Greek frozen yogurt. They're jumping on the trend that has seen smoother, higher-protein Greek yogurt double sales in each of the past three years. It's still not "that" healthy, of course,

"What tools do I need to be an innovator?" My answer was simple and for many, surprising: "Your eyes and ears."

Whether you're a product developer, retailer, manufacturer or service provider, you too can uncover the little discoveries and everyday surprises that engage today's consumers, who are always looking for something new, different, better and fun.

but Ben & Jerry's positions it as a "reasonable reward," not health food. It's a fast, clever move to harness consumers' changing tastes and growing health concerns, while maintaining Ben & Jerry's reputation for flamboyant branding. Who else would sell Greek frozen yogurt in flavors such as Strawberry Shortcake, Raspberry Fudge Chunk and Banana Peanut Butter?

Second, I observed a large billboard for the successful A&E TV show, Storage Wars. It's about modern-day treasure hunters, competing to acquire abandoned storage lockers that might conceal antiques, collectibles, bargains and other forgotten treasures. Why do people love this reality show? Both the idea and the timing were right. It's about discovery, at a time when millions find themselves in tough economic circumstances. It's an adult version of a kid's game, deeply rooted in fond memories. This combination of hope, fun, triumph and even disappointment has become an elixir to lighten people's daily struggles. Again, the simple matching of an idea that reflects people's wants and needs becomes an innovation.

Little discoveries and everyday surprises

The point is this: Whether you're a product developer, retailer, manufacturer or service provider, you too can uncover the little discoveries and everyday surprises that engage today's consumers, who are always looking for something new, different, better and fun.

What we see depends mainly on what we look for.
Sir John Lubbock

Next time you're in another city — or just a new part of your town — don't think of sitting back in a cab or going underground in the subway. Take a walk. Look up, look down, look around, notice what people are wearing, doing, enjoying. Venture into stores you wouldn't normally go into. The more you leave the office to see and hear other people, products, places and new approaches, the more you will see what consumers are doing – and the more ideas you will gather to make your own work more innovative. Plus, a walk is good for your health.

Throughout this book, you are going to be peppered with ideas and examples like these, many of which were uncovered by simply being aware of what's going on around us. A number of themes will emerge as we cover the key factors that help you become a successful innovator.

- We explore what innovation is and how to identify the many simple opportunities for innovation that surround us day-to-day.

- We look at companies with consumer-focused platforms and processes (Starbucks, Apple, Disney) that are different from those of commodity-based companies (makers of coffee or computers, or suppliers of personal or business services), and discuss how great companies create more opportunities to be innovative.

- We show you how to shift your mindset from thinking like a commodity provider to thinking like a platform builder.

- We expose the misconception that innovation equals invention, which will help you understand how accessible and powerful innovation can be.

- We show you how innovation can change your business in small simple steps by walking you through the 90% Rule®, which helps you create a dynamic, customer-focused culture of innovation in your business.

The 90% Rule is a straightforward philosophy that recognizes that, when it comes to introducing successful new innovations, you are already 90% of the way there. It gets you to leverage the 90% of the work that you already understand or are capable of doing, and then constantly ask, "What's the next 10%?" What's the next product, service or process improvement that will create a continuously engaged customer base, strengthen your brand and grow the business?

Keep in mind that while I emphasize that innovation is easy, it does require some effort, a change of thinking, and constant commitment. But then, what doesn't?

He has the deed half done who has made a beginning.

Horace

If you are one of those people who get out of bed every morning to make a difference, your commitment to innovation is alive and well. And if your energy is rooted in audacity, you're ahead of the game. To some, audacity may be a negative concept associated with attitude or edge, but the real definition centers on the willingness to challenge assumptions and conventions – and that's the catalyst for innovation. Often, the biggest challenge of innovation is to overcome two well-known barriers to change: the naysayers in the room who say, "That'll never work, because...." and those who say, "We don't have time to innovate."

Make it work. If you don't, your competitors will.

Ready to cause a disturbance? Read on.

Simplifying Innovation: Don't Forget to Change the Oil

The goal of innovation is to keep things fresh in your business, so that your customers have reasons to keep coming back.

John Paulo Cardoso

You wouldn't change the oil in your car just once a year – the engine would sputter, seize up and die. So why let your company leave innovation or the introduction of new – even small – improvements to an annual schedule, planned retreats or sporadic brainstorming? Tune up your innovation engine regularly and keep it running. Or ignore it and let your business sputter, maybe even seize up and die.

Marry once; innovate forever

Every bride wants her wedding to be special (grooms too … usually). Engaged couples scour magazines, catalogues, stores and movies to find just the right props, decorations, themes and accessories to ensure their wedding is an eye-popping celebration of their uniqueness and love.

You wouldn't change the oil in your car just once a year – the engine would sputter, seize up and die. So why let your company leave innovation or the introduction of new – even small – improvements to an annual schedule, planned retreats or sporadic brainstorming?

Weddingstar understands that a wedding happens just once, but the innovative thinking that goes into it is — must be — endless. They know innovative ideas can come from anywhere, all of the time. That's what fuels the growth of this fast-growing, Canadian-based international company from the prairie city of Medicine Hat, Alberta, population 60,000. Weddingstar is dedicated to product innovation. Want a "caketopper" for the top of your wedding cake that features a bride and groom bowling, playing rugby, or locked in a passionate kiss? Weddingstar provides it. Want the groom to have black hair and the bride to have red? Weddingstar does it.

Weddingstar founder and CEO Rick Brink says, "Every bride is looking for something different, something unique and personal. And Weddingstar sells in over 70 countries, offering more than 3,000 products — 90% of them developed by our own in-house design team." You name it: Diamond-shaped tea-light holders, personalized imprinted ribbons, engraved crystal champagne glasses, intricately die-cut and personalized name cards, cupcake wraps, and various styles and colors of metal birdcages for holding candles, name cards or gift envelopes. Weddingstar offers so many products that no one retailer could stock them all, and too many variations to browse through even on the Web, so Weddingstar has also entered the publishing business, producing a magazine/catalogue that sells for $9.99 on newsstands across North America.

Like many businesses, Weddingstar got started "by accident" — an entrepreneurial opportunity. In 1982 Rick Brink was playing professional hockey in Denmark while looking for a business to bring back to his native Canada. He decided to import a line of "honeycomb" party supplies — paper figures of Santa Claus, Easter bunnies, clowns and cowboys that swing open like a book into eye-catching 3-D decorations. Showing his samples to prospective customers, Brink listened when one retailer asked for pop-up wedding bells in three colors, pink, white and lavender. While most of Brink's inventory languished in stores, those bells took off. He decided he was in the wedding business.

Line by line, Brink grew his product offering, adding more accessories such as streamers, candles and confetti cards. But most of these products were similar to those of his competitors, and when Weddingstar started to gain traction its rivals responded with a price war that nearly put Brink out of business. "That made me realize that I had to be different from everyone else," he says. "To stay in business we had to innovate."

By offering more unique products and sky's-the-limit customized options, including higher-end pillows, garters and guestbooks (many produced locally by skilled crafters), Weddingstar climbed out of the commodity bog and created its own category. An added advantage for prices and margins was that budget-conscious consumers couldn't compare prices – because no one offered the products that Weddingstar did. As a result, says Brink, "Pricing is not a threat to us anymore."

Innovative product ideas come from everywhere. Patricia MacArthur, Weddingstar's executive creative director, like an anxious bride, pores over catalogues and magazines for new product ideas. The company also keeps up with manufacturing technology, particularly new printing equipment that enables it to personalize everything from banners to wine glasses. One of Weddingstar's most popular products, a "sand ceremony" kit (in which bride and groom pour colored sands into a single vessel to symbolize their union), came from spotting a similar ceremony on TV's The Bachelor. Brink is now hiring design-school graduates to give his company more ability to create on the fly.

Think about it: customers are engaged by "new." New and exciting products, new and better services, new announcements about their favorite brands, new advances by their preferred companies. "New" reinforces their buying decisions, reconfirms their preferences and gives them reason to buy again and again.

As Weddingstar's brand grows, more rivals are copying its products. So Brink has only a slim, single-season lead over the competition. It's innovate, innovate, innovate. Fortunately, success also brings more opportunities. Weddingstar recently teamed up to produce signature tabletop accessories designed by celebrity New York wedding planner Preston Bailey, whose A-list clients include Donald Trump, Liza Minnelli, and Michael Douglas and Catherine Zeta-Jones. Similarly, the company has been offered distribution rights for products from Beverly Clark, one of the biggest names in wedding products. "Beverly Clark is a company I was dying to get hold of in my early days," says Brink. "Now we've come full circle and they are after us to carry their product." Innovation opportunities come in many forms; the more experience and success you have, the more often they knock on your door.

Ideas are like wheelbarrows.
They stand still until someone pushes them.

Unknown

Like the people at Weddingstar, you need to believe that innovation is the engine that drives your business forward – and it doesn't run well in spits and starts. It needs to be a well-oiled machine, constantly serving your customers. Think about it: customers are engaged by "new." New and exciting products, new and better services, new announcements about their favorite brands, new advances by their preferred companies. "New" reinforces their buying decisions, reconfirms their preferences and gives them reason to buy again and again. More importantly, in today's overcrowded marketplace, it gives them something to talk about. And "customer talk" courses through the veins of the marketplace these days as if it were the lifeblood of consumer decision-making. The old adage that there's nothing as powerful as word-of-mouth has whole new meaning in today's globally connected markets. The Internet and the digital sphere offer innovators an ever-expanding landscape of opportunity, a place where millions of people can "like," "share," "tweet," "pin" (on Pinterest) and "buzz" (on Buzzfeed) about the latest and greatest. Your innovative ideas, new products and new add-ons can get you into the conversation, and the more you innovate the more you will be talked about.

Today—not sometime later this year—you must make innovation a continuous, front-burner activity, as important as your most vital activities, from sales and marketing to production and finance. In fact, innovation should be embedded in all these operations, too.

A year from now you may wish you had started today.

Karen Lamb

Do it!

When I ask business owners and managers about innovation, many of them talk about ideas they have percolating, but which they never find time to get to. The most common roadblock? They're too busy fighting front-burner issues to get around to anything new. If you know you're not innovating constantly, this is probably your number one excuse too. If you want innovation to be a source of new products, revenue and growth then I have three words for you, from one of the world's most innovative companies. "Just Do It." It's as simple as that. You do not need to reinvent, just rethink. And do it.

Innovation is about bringing ideas to market rather than letting them languish on a half-forgotten scratchpad or the back of an easily misplaced napkin. Good ideas do not need to languish or be lost. Just a little bit of new thinking and new doing will bring them to fruition.

Innovation is about bringing ideas to market rather than letting them languish on a half-forgotten scratchpad or the back of an easily misplaced napkin.

Five minutes of today are worth more time than five minutes in the next millennium.

Ralph Waldo Emerson

One of the reasons good ideas are left unattended is because the idea of innovation gets mixed up with the idea of invention; consequently, making a mountain out of a mole hill. Innovation is not invention, because it's not simply about creation; it's about commercialization. It's about successfully bringing ideas – some small, some big – to market with ingenuity and rigor. Another impediment to new ideas is the fear of change, which can transform great ideas into a giant pile of procrastination. Innovation is not a holy grail to be rediscovered every now and then. Rather, it is about continually uncovering opportunities that you can embrace now. They are there, right in front of you, waiting to be discovered amid the grist and grind of getting the work done.

Jonathan Swift once said, "Necessity is the mother of invention." Mark Twain said, "Necessity is the mother of taking chances." I say, "Innovation is the necessary mother of success." Innovation is about thinking and acting on opportunities that are already there, and about adapting existing solutions for other applications, markets or industries. You don't have to invent anything or reinvent the wheel; just turn it, slightly, in a different direction. And you can do that 52 weeks a year.

Take the first steps

A journey of a thousand miles starts with one step.

Lao-tzu

Winning through innovation – some call it "win-novation" – doesn't have to be scary, painful or expensive. Done right, it's easy, and grows step by step. It starts with two things:

1) *First, you need a process that allows ideas to come forward and be considered, and then ensures the best are implemented.* This can be done on a very manageable scale; if you allow it to happen, ideas will rise out of the depths of your organization. The barrier is that there is usually no process for bringing ideas into the light of day, so they fall by the wayside, remaining unexplored thoughts in employees' minds and forgotten notes on a scratchpad.

2) *Second, you need to create an environment in which employees, trusted partners, even customers, willingly suggest new ideas.* Again, it's not difficult if you have a process in place. For example, an electronic suggestion box is a good idea *if* it's part of a process that actually processes suggestions – all of them. Too often, suggestion boxes become inboxes stuffed with good ideas but unconnected to a dedicated innovation process. So when the majority of suggestions aren't properly processed – and feedback provided – the chance of creating an innovative environment dries up, along with all the suggestions. Soon the box is an empty reminder of what innovation is not. (The same is true for sporadic brainstorming sessions that are not part of a broader process.)

The right process and the right environment go hand in hand. There needs to be an engaging, encouraging, open environment, with a clear, tangible and transparent process that runs throughout the company.

It's not complex. The cost is low. The potential is sky-high.

Try this

Remember, it's better to implement a number of small innovations than wait for big ideas that you never get around to. Also, people, especially at first, are more receptive to incremental rather than wholesale change; in the early stages, a few small initiatives will help move the innovation needle. Here's one example of what you can try as a first step.

Set aside a 15-minute slot in your weekly sales and marketing meeting. Ask everyone at the table to talk about one interesting innovation they have seen in your industry, or better yet, an industry far from your own. Discuss which examples are most applicable to your business, then charge a person or a small team to flesh out those next ideas. Monitor their progress regularly (weekly and/or monthly) in subsequent meetings. You will be amazed at what unfolds. Success will breed success, and positive feedback will stimulate even more and more ideas. This first step in the process will create new thinking, engagement and inclusiveness, which are the lifeblood of innovation. And once it starts pumping through your organization, innovation becomes infectious.

> ### The man who removes a mountain begins by carrying away small stones.
> *William Faulkner*

As a relentless advocate and cheerleader for innovation, I continually harp on its importance as a stimulus for organic growth and competitive advantage. What I sometimes forget to say is that innovation is also fun. It's always rewarding to change the status quo, cause a disturbance and upset the "melon cart" (more on that later). And, of course, the real fun is watching your customers enjoying something new – and buying more!

... people, especially at first, are more receptive to incremental rather than wholesale change; in the early stages, a few small initiatives will help move the innovation needle.

Chapter **3**

Innovation Drives Marketing and Sales

Markets change, customers change, tastes change. Companies that want to compete in ever-changing markets had better learn how to change, too.

Ken Tencer

Sooner or later, you have to sell something. I would like to help you make the register ring sooner – and more frequently. In order to do that, you need to reconsider the foundational continuum of business growth: innovation, marketing and sales.

INNOVATION > MARKETING > SALES = GROWTH

Where do we start? I like to start with childhood, because the perspective from those halcyon days makes an ideal metaphor for the reality we experience when we grow up. Somewhere between childhood and adulthood we learned that the world is neither predictable nor what we thought it would be. Remember when you were young? We were told we would be part of the leisure class, live in a 'paperless society' and have a few mammoth computers like "Big Blue" and Univac running our businesses. We were told that technology would

Sooner or later, you have to sell something. I would like to help you make the register ring sooner – and more frequently.

help us organize better, do things faster, and save us time and money. And we were "promised" a four-day workweek. But a funny thing happened on the way to the twenty-first century. It never happened. Instead, technology has delivered a 24/7/365 reality. The promise of long, leisurely weekends? Gone like our childhood. The reality? Technology has given us a never-ending day with incessant access, universal connections and a massive overdose of information.

Business is in perpetual motion: up, down, sideways, backward, forward. Never still. But regardless of the direction, there's always too much to do with too few resources. Add to that the most recent tsunami of economic reality, and we find ourselves in the most uncertain times since our childhood. Some say since the Great Depression. Worse, we don't know what's around the corner, let alone over the horizon. A 2012 Gallup Poll found that 30% of American workers are worried about their jobs. Global uncertainty seriously encumbers businesses from doing what businesses do best: investing in the future. Business owners and executives are stuck in a holding pattern, waiting for something to happen. And yet we instinctively know that we must make things happen ourselves; we must find new ways of doing things.

New products and services are what drive growth, generate jobs, open new markets and create new processes, experiences and possibilities that were never dreamed of in our childhood. This is no time to rest on our laurels or stay "on hold." If we want growth, we must invest now.

Business, more than any other occupation,
is a continual dealing with the future;
it is a continual calculation,
an instinctive exercise in foresight.

Henry Luce

Somewhere between childhood and adulthood we learned that the world is neither predictable nor what we thought it would be.

Customers are central to every business and every business model. Keeping them engaged with "new, better and exciting" is paramount; therefore, bringing "new, better and exciting" to market is imperative. This is the essence of innovation. If you are marketing and selling the "same old, same old" you cannot sustain growth.

What drives growth?

For decades there has been an ongoing debate between marketing and sales as to which one drives growth more. I say, it's no contest. *Innovation* drives marketing, which, in turn, drives sales. Why? Because marketing and sales depend on innovation. It starts with innovation, not the other way around.

Think about it. Customers are central to every business and every business model. Keeping them engaged with "new, better and exciting" is paramount; therefore, bringing "new, better and exciting" to market is imperative. This is the essence of innovation. If you are marketing and selling the "same old, same old" you cannot sustain growth. If innovation is not inextricably tied to marketing and sales, growth will stagnate. Guaranteed.

Want a great example? Look at the beauty industry. Every season the powerful, global brands come out with new products, cases, fragrances, promotions, colors, spokespeople, events ... the list is endless. Why? Beauty is fickle. It is the perception of the moment. If any one of those companies rested on last year's laurels, they would fall behind in one season. The same is true for Weddingstar. They know very well that we cannot leave innovation – the most powerful force in this triumvirate – to sporadic once-in-a-while events of hope and change. It must be an integrated part of every process that runs through a company. Innovation must become as natural to business owners, managers and employees as sales and marketing.

The two pillars of business growth are actually a tripod.

Since this book focuses on the new mantra of innovation, I want to talk a little more about what I call the three pillars of business: innovation, marketing and sales. To be successful, these three disciplines must work together, and not languish as separate silos. Success requires assimilated thinking and functionality. I spend a great deal of time inside many client businesses, and I am continually disappointed at how separate sales and marketing are, and how divorced innovation is from both.

Marketing 101 clearly sets out:

- The purpose of marketing is to identify and qualify markets and customers; develop products and/or services; map the road to market; and define and create effective communications.

- The purpose of sales is to develop customer relations; deliver the force behind "closing sales"; provide important market feedback; and directly impact the top-line and middle-line gross margins.

Marketing 101 is unusually silent on the critical third leg of growth, innovation.

First, it's important to ensure that the collective thinking throughout the company understands that investing in marketing is as important as investing in sales. Together they can be a significant point of leverage; managed separately, they offer more dysfunction than leverage, and exacerbate the disconnect with customers. And until the "twin" relationship is strategically connected to the third leg of innovation, growth will be stunted.

> ### Everything I ever needed to know about selling ... was learning how to identify, find and keep customers.
>
> *Lillian Vernon, Catalogue retailer*

Business colleague and "the Sales Growth Expert" Adrian Davis, for whom I have a high regard, has written extensively on the importance of marketing and sales working hand in hand. To better understand the role innovation has to play with these two disciplines let's explore some of Adrian's thinking.

Historically, there has been a divide between sales and marketing. Many companies have yet to get their sales and marketing teams working together seamlessly, whether business-to-business or consumer sales. However, the new economy – the new reality – is forcing the issue with more economic pressure, more demanding buyers, more niche competitors, more short-life products and longer sales cycles. Sales people are being forced to think more like marketers and marketing people are being forced to think more like sales people. And that's a good thing.

One good funnel leads to another

Both sales and marketing have their own funnels. Marketing must directly tie the end of their funnel to the beginning of the sales funnel. Moreover, the output of the sales funnel must tie back into the marketing funnel. Every dollar spent on marketing must be measurable and show a return on investment, and every lead generated for the sales force must be accounted for and show its return on investment. Marketing that only focuses on understanding the markets and creating awareness in the marketplace doesn't work for most companies. Today, most CEOs and CFOs must get more from their marketing, and the good marketing executives get ahead of this scrutiny by making marketing a major point of leverage.

Measure everything

They do so by carefully planning their sales and marketing programs and campaigns, and setting up clear measurement criteria to determine which programs and campaigns are successful, and how to increase their effectiveness over time. To measure these factors, marketers must clearly track all activity through the marketing funnel to the sales funnel. The marketing funnel should consist of three key stages:

1. Reach: The number of people in the potential base that will be touched by specific sales and marketing programs.
2. Enquiry: The number of people who respond positively by initiating contact.
3. Who buys: In consumer sales and business-to-business.

Linking funnels

The marketing funnel is directly linked to the sales funnel. In business-to-business, first meetings represent the top of the sales funnel. All activities prior to the first meeting represent part of the marketing funnel, which sales people should be engaged in. Once a first meeting is successfully concluded, the sales funnel should comprise three key stages:

1. Diagnose: The buyer is willing to work with the sales professional to help better understand the situation and develop a solution.
2. Propose: The consumer is clear on why they should buy. Or the B2B buyer is clear about the challenge they are facing and what your firm can do about it, and is open to receiving clear documentation on the way you can work with them to fill their needs.
3. Close: The buyer, ready to take action to resolve the challenges, is now negotiating and completing necessary paperwork to initiate a purchase.

Wash, rinse, repeat

The end of the sales funnel is the beginning of the marketing funnel (surprise!). Marketing must now engage in programs that reach and re-engage the entire customer base – existing and prospects – to help to drive future sales.

To do so, sales and marketing must also meet to discuss **new** products, services and processes to engage both the existing and prospective customers.

With this one three-letter word, **new**, we have now completed the loop and intuitively added the third pillar to our growth strategy, innovation – the new, improved, better and different that delights the customer. It is the instinctive, unnamed pillar that many companies have undertaken for years, but neither defined nor put to process. In today's business world, we need to do both to succeed. Haphazard, undisciplined ideation accompanied by spotty implementation does not cut it.

Small becomes big by linking innovation, marketing & sales

One small company that has made the leap to a disciplined growth strategy and broken into new markets is OMI Industries of Chicago.

What OMI understood was that simple innovation can lead to retargeting the same product to a different market and drive sales growth. This effort can be tricky, because you have to unlearn many of the things that worked in one market in order to determine what works in the next. OMI made this leap. It took the same deodorizing technology it developed for refineries, landfills and sewage plants and turned it into a "green" consumer product sold in high-end boutiques and specialty chains such as Ace Hardware, Whole Foods and Bed Bath & Beyond. Whether its customers are manufacturers, asphalt producers, pet owners or cigar smokers, "all buy the same technology," says OMI president Phil Coffey. "Just in different forms."

Originally known as Odor Management Inc., OMI discovered a formula for using natural plant oils such as lime, anise seed, cedar and clove to attract and break down malodorous molecules. OMI's Ecosorb® products actually eliminate bad smells, rather than mask them as most air fresheners do. OMI built a small but profitable business serving industrial clients until Coffey joined the company and suggested it explore consumer markets. He needed to convince the then-owners, because they saw OMI as an industrial products company, while Coffey saw it as an innovator whose brands could reach every household in America.

He knew the job would be tough. Ecosorb would have to be reformulated into scores of different products. Instead of meeting clients one-on-one through plant visits or trade shows, the company would have to create new relationships with wholesalers and retailers.

In 2003, Coffey prepared his staff for the makeover by warning they could expect no raises for the next three years – and offering shares in the company as an incentive. He then poured all of OMI's profits into producing new "Fresh Wave®" products (gels, candles, sprays, laundry additives and pet shampoos), with eye-catching packaging. By 2005, the brand could be found in 3,000 stores; by 2009 it was in 10,000.

And there was more. Developing new products for its industrial markets by becoming marketing-focused and innovative helped OMI sell to major commercial businesses. In mid-2009 Hertz Car rental began using Fresh Wave products to neutralize rental-car odors at 1200 locations.

A Hertz spokesman said, "The technology OMI is providing us will enable us to keep our cars on the road longer. We'll have less downtime due to cleaning issues." (And fewer customer complaints about lingering food and tobacco smells.)

As OMI clearly demonstrated, when a new growth strategy is undertaken – requiring innovation – it is imperative that sales and marketing, and other disciplines, recognize they are part of the same process and work seamlessly in pursuit of innovation at every turn. It's obvious that sales and marketing needs to deliver continuous customer engagement, which is driven by innovation. And yet, I see too many companies focusing just on sales results, and pushing innovation, the engine that drives the future, to a once-a-year annual retreat.

> **If you want to innovate, to change an enterprise or a society, it takes people willing to do what's not expected.**
>
> *Jean Riboud, French Industrialist*

Want a quick and easy set of questions to keep you on-track and thinking innovatively every day? Each morning I ask myself three things:

1) What am I going to sell today? I start with this because, as I said at the start of the chapter, you have to sell something!

2) What *one thing* am I going to do differently today? I highlight *one* thing because I (and probably you) need to choose just one activity or process, not many, and focus on it to drive successful change.

3) How do the answers to the first two questions tie in to my company's long-term strategy? This helps me stay on-course and not chase shiny, short-term opportunities that take me and the business off-track.

These simple questions help you coalesce your thinking around vision, strategy and opportunities, and serve as a constant reminder that innovation generated by paying attention to customer delight is the engine that drives growth.

I will act now for now is all I have. Tomorrow is the day reserved for the labor of the lazy ... Success will not wait. If I delay, success will become wed to another and lost to me forever.

Og Mandino, author, The World's Greatest Salesman

Chapter 4

Understanding innovation: process, product and service

Process innovation frees up cash, which gets invested in new products and services, which delights customers. It's a winning formula.

Ken Tencer

I said in the title of the first chapter that innovation sounds difficult. Now, I want tell you — somewhat cryptically — why it is *not*: If you can slice a melon or make a right-hand turn, you can be a breakthrough innovator.

Generally speaking, there are two categories of innovation, simple and disruptive. Simple innovation starts at one end of the innovation spectrum and moves along a continuum, aggregating into disruptive innovation at the other end.

Simple or "simple-adaptive" innovation begins with you being able to recognize the obvious. The "cake pop" in front of you. The Coca-Cola freestyle in your midst. Or the paint and primer all-in-one can. In other words, It's about seeing the obvious and adapting. In the past few years, Coca-Cola finally recognized what kids have been doing for generations; mixing other drinks and flavored syrups to customize their Coke. Now kids everywhere are flocking to specific McDonald's, Burger King, Wendy's and Five Guys restaurants equipped with Coke's 100+ flavor freestyle drink machine – which lets them mix and match their favorite flavors from Coke, Fanta, Minute Maid, Dr. Pepper and other Coca-Cola brands. The obvious, however, is only obvious after the fact. Otherwise, why did it take so long for paint manufacturers such as Behr to develop line of paints that have the primer mixed right in? Where was that obvious add-on when I was painting the kids' rooms?

The best companies turn innovation into a continuum that grows and evolves along with their customers: think Coke to Diet Coke to Diet Cherry Coke to Coca-Cola freestyle. Simple-adaptive innovation results in one-off ideas that help your business move forward in smaller, near-term steps. Focused-disruptive innovation creates a continuous stream of focused "next-step" innovations, as well as a longer-term thought process for introducing and adapting innovation into your markets. Focused-disruptive innovation creates a complete platform for continuous innovation, disruption and market dominance. Understanding the process of continuously leading and delighting your customers is the market magic that separates Oprah from Rosie and Disney from fall fairs.

We'll delve more deeply into this innovation continuum – from simple-adaptive to focused-disruptive - in the next chapter. But first let's understand the types of innovation that drive the continuum – process, products and services.

Don't just read this book, live it – it's all process

You need to begin the process of innovation with divergent thinking. In other words, get out of the office and out of your norms. See what other industries are doing and where the world around you is going. The clues are everywhere.

Divergent thinking can be – and should be – employed at all times, in all situations, including while you're reading this book. Divergent thoughts are where new ideas live. As we share ideas throughout this book, you will get a taste of how divergent thought is part of a process that leads to more innovation. With an innovative mind-set and divergent thinking, you will find yourself dreaming up all kinds of new, unsettling, ridiculous and highly promising ideas. As we tell you recent stories of successful innovations and reveal what the innovation masters are doing, you should be spurred to put together divergent concepts of your own, generate new ideas, and quickly evaluate them for how they might fit with your company and its culture, its capabilities, and its customers. By the time you're finished the book, you should have a scratchpad full of ideas well worth investigating. So have a pen handy and make copious notes.

The two faces of innovation: process and products/services

Too many people think that innovation is limited to breakthrough products or services. It is not. In fact, *process innovation* – finding faster, cheaper and better ways to deliver your products and services to customers - can bring you a significant competitive advantage, substantial savings all while building brand equity – because there is no better way to delight your customer than by delivering faster, with better quality.

It is important to understand the difference between process innovation and products and services innovation.

- Product and service innovation is about bringing improvements, incremental or big, to your products or services – or adding new ones – in order to attract new customers and improve revenues and growth.

With an innovative mind-set and divergent thinking, you will find yourself dreaming up all kinds of new, unsettling, ridiculous and highly promising ideas.

- Process innovation looks at how you produce and deliver your products and services — everything from engineering and marketing to delivery and finance. It's about finding ways within the process to do things better, differently and more efficiently in order to save time, money and improve the delivery of your products and services.

Process innovation can be as easy as not making a phone call. Here is an example of how, in a small way, we recently answered the process challenge in my company. I began to use LinkedIn to source freelance branding and graphic design rather than calling a traditional staffing agency. For a cost of under $300 an ad, I received over 100 responses, beginning in less than one hour. I was also able to negotiate hourly rates that were about $10 an hour *lower* than I had been paying to agencies as their commission. So in the first week, worst case, I was ahead — saving $10 an hour for 35 hours or $350 for the week. This process innovation enabled me to fill staffing requirements more quickly and created savings that I reinvested in growth-driven opportunities.

It's the process – not products or services – that gives an organization an extraordinary competitive edge.

Philip Kirby, Managing Partner, OTI Inc. and author of
Thoughtware®: Change the Thinking & the Organization
Will Change Itself

Philip Kirby, a business colleague and a specialist in organizational change, says that the amount of cost savings available in a company's processes is enormous. He tells his clients that he can improve their performance, "guaranteed" — and he delivers. He achieves these results by improving the company's processes, and he has done this on a global basis for more than 20 years. Here are a few examples of the results he has produced:

- Throughput gains from 10% to 75% across eight processes,
- 50% reduction in the time required to build a product,
- 98% improvement in cycle time,
- 93% reduction in registration processing time.

Philip's firm has an innovative way of looking at, seeing and thinking about each client's business. He calls it the "primacy of process," and demonstrates that the critical link between customers and profits is process. The results speak volumes.

I was recently speaking at a conference on innovation. Over the three days, I only remember one example of process innovation being described by the presenters -- everyone was focused on products and services. Hey, nothing wrong with creating better products and services. But let's not forget that the processes through which you design a product, engineer it, make it, store it, ship it, deliver it, service it and finance it have a huge impact on costs and thus profits, not to mention creating delight (or displeasure) in your customers. All of these processes can make your products or services better or worse, cheaper or more expensive, depending on how efficient and effective they are. There are enormous hidden costs buried in processes, and innovative thinking is the key to uncovering them. Done right, it can be a new and significant source of financing. At the conference, the one example of process innovation that stuck with me concerned a large company that managed to re-engineer their to-market supply chain in order to improve cash flow – cash they used to fund new customer-driven initiatives. That is how process innovation becomes a new source of financing which, in turn, can be invested in product and service innovation.

When it comes to finance, particularly cost savings, it's important to understand the difference between process innovation and the good old "slash and burn" method of boosting cash flow. In every organization, processes have a significant impact on costs: purchasing, inventories, reworking, downtime, lead-time, material travel time, delivery time, wasted time, and so on. All these processes add costs, which means they provide a wealth of opportunities for hefty savings. When you come up with new ways of improving throughput or order processing, or reducing wait-times and delivery times, it's found money. Philip Kirby calls it "hidden treasure."

Let me be clear. I'm not suggesting you stop thoughtful, rigorous cost-cutting. But in tough times, urgent reactive cost-cutting is too often shortsighted and arbitrary, done to appease stakeholders, shareholders and short-term quarterly reports. Unfortunately, the long-term consequences aren't usually factored into the equation. It's an accounting exercise — cut budgets, trim fat, do less or do it less well. Doing more with less is possible, but it usually comes from a strategic approach to process, not quick-fix cutbacks. Too often, companies cut their way into bigger problems as they deliver less service, reduce customer satisfaction, undermine brand value, lose market share, and sacrifice growth for the appearance of efficiency. These steps almost always lead in the wrong direction, and hurt the company. Of course, costs must be cut, but the real goal should be to *cut costs while driving growth*. It can be done, and the place to start is with your processes. It starts by understanding that there is great waste in your current processes, but where it's buried is not always obvious. And by ensuring that the entire organization understands that *innovation can be both the company's biggest cost-saving strategy and its best growth strategy.*

When it comes to finance, particularly cost savings, it's important to understand the difference between process innovation and the good old "slash and burn" method of boosting cash flow.

I want you to think of process innovation as another means of lowering costs, building efficiencies and increasing output. Process innovations can be self-funding and free up cash for product and service innovation. It's a double win. One other point: Process innovation can be easy and quick because it includes countless small opportunities seen every day that every company, big or small, can do right away.

Take a right-hand turn

For process innovation at street-level, there is no better example than United Parcel Service (UPS). UPS's right-hand turn innovation is brilliant. In 2005 the company adopted a new route-optimization system that eliminated time-sucking and potentially risky left-hand turns. This system enabled drivers to drive fewer miles, decrease delivery times, reduce fuel consumption and reduce accidents (more accidents happen when making left-hand turns). Overall, this single innovation produced higher revenue per driver and vehicle.

Just think of the time and money your business could save through the application of business process software in such areas as marketing, research, recruiting, project management, and online video and conference calling – applications that now let even the smallest companies run on-line marketing, ask questions, find employees, or engage co-workers and collaborators from around the world, instantly from the comfort of your office (or living room).

> **Be like a turtle ... If it didn't stick its neck out, it wouldn't get anywhere at all.**
>
> *Harvey Mackay, author of Dig Your Well Before You're Thirsty*

My challenge to you is to *first* rethink your processes and uncover cost-saving opportunities that are hiding in broad

My challenge to you is to *first* rethink your processes and uncover cost-saving opportunities that are hiding in broad daylight, waiting for new thinking. Realize the savings and then reinvest your newfound cash to create market-engaging breakthroughs in product and service innovations.

daylight, waiting for new thinking. Realize the savings and then reinvest your newfound cash to create market-engaging breakthroughs in product and service innovations. In finance, don't myopically try to cut your way to the bottom line by doing more with less. That's not improving the bottom line, it's moving to the back of the line. Demand more innovative thinking that moves you to the front of the line and enhances your bottom line with higher sales, not temporarily lowered costs.

The innovation challenge

Earlier I said, "Don't just read this book, live it." Here's a first step that will make you understand the power and simplicity of innovation, as well as demonstrate how it can help finance itself. In fact, innovation can be, without a doubt, the easiest, least expensive and most productive way of investing in your business' future. As mentioned – but worth repeating – it can increase throughput, output and productivity *while lowering costs*. That's an equation you shouldn't ignore. Wouldn't it be better to find new ways to make budget without costly cutbacks and layoffs, which usually undermine your opportunity to grow?

The innovation challenge – your challenge – is to use process innovation as a reinvestment strategy by cutting costs and improving productivity, and then developing new cash-producing products and services that grow the business.

Essentially, I am asking you to challenge your people to look at how your products and services are made, supported and brought to market.

Think very simple (for now). Think LinkedIn. Right-hand turns. Video conferencing. Online research using free or low-cost tools such as SurveyMonkey.

Even this simple exercise demands blue-sky thinking, and the generation of many ideas. Follow that by developing a filtering mechanism (criteria) that lets your team decide which one opportunity makes the most sense to pursue. And, of course, don't forget to set goals and report back your progress to the team.

This entire process is rooted in (and begins to develop) three skills:

1. How to identify innovative opportunities.
2. How to filter the opportunities.
3. How to implement the best ones.

While we have limited this exercise to simple process innovation for now, these three skills are embedded in all forms of innovation. They serve as the heart and foundation of six steps of The 90% Rule, which we explore in Part III.

Chapter 5

The Innovation Continuum: From Simple to Disruptive

Anybody can do what Apple, Oprah, Dove, UPS, and OMI do. To disrupt your market, however, first you must disrupt the conventional thinking that got you there.

John Paulo Cardoso

In the previous chapter I talked about the types of innovation, and introduced the notion of innovation as a continuum with two general categories or types of innovation: 1) Simple-adaptive; and 2) Focused-disruptive. Now let's jump in.

Simple-adaptive innovation is about making basic adaptations to your existing products or services in order to further delight current customers or attract new ones.

The late John Kenneth Galbraith (1908–2006) once said, "A person buying ordinary products in a supermarket is in touch with his deepest emotions." The renowned economist was highlighting the intrinsic connection between people's fundamental emotional needs and their everyday buying decisions, from groceries and fast-food to big-screen TVs and SUVs. Customers don't always "know" exactly what

If you pay close attention and look, listen and learn, you will see many opportunities to continually renew your engagement with customers.

they want as they choose between products and services and endlessly "new" offerings from marketers. But if you pay close attention and look, listen and learn, you will see many opportunities to continually renew your engagement with customers. The customer's decision to buy – or not – is inextricably linked to your decision to innovate – or not. A few years ago, the decisions made by supermarket customers were a big part of some fresh innovation in an industry that primarily offers commodity products and services.

Melons for all

Supermarket innovation has been wide-ranging, from store design and shopping experience to product offering and distribution. But perhaps the most obvious example of simple-adaptive but dramatic innovation – and one of my favorites – is captured in my tongue-in-cheek accolade to the supermarket industry.

"If you can slice a melon, you can be a breakthrough innovator."

In the wake of hectic go-go lifestyles that saw an increasing trend to prepared and take-out foods, grocers made a play to own this new category. They created a vast, affordable new product selection that ranges from fresh melon slices to fully cooked meals-to-go. When supermarkets started offering ready-to-eat foods, it was one of those "obvious-in-hindsight, virtuoso-in-foresight" ideas that make you ask, "Why didn't we think of that?"

My answer: Because you were not looking for simple-adaptive innovation. And you didn't understand two critical principles:

1) Innovation is more readily available to you than you believe.

2) Innovation is about causing a disturbance in the marketplace, and it starts by changing the status quo.

Innovation is an uphill climb for many – a Mount Everest for some – because they think it means "invention" – and major upheaval. The truth couldn't be more different. That's why understanding simple-adaptive is so important. There are so many innovators who prove that innovation is not just the preserve of big companies. In fact, much innovation comes from "small" – from small ideas and small efforts started in many small corners of an organization. Over the past 30 years we have all marveled at the innovation in information technology and yet, the evolution of computers has been more incremental (simple-adaptive) than big breakthrough (focused-disruptive). Most of the time, innovation is about simply adapting what already is. And the lesson is clear and observable: Anybody can do it.

Genius is the ability to reduce the complicated to the simple.

C. W. Ceram

Adapt, adapt, adapt

Companies everywhere – well, the smart ones – are employing simple-adaptive innovation every imaginable way. Here are a few inspiring examples that became huge successes. Some of these I covered in a series of columns that I wrote for Canada's national newspaper, The Globe and Mail.

Seeing the same thing in a different way

Think of the publicity coup for Post's Shreddies (plus its 18-point gain in market share) when it reintroduced the timeless breakfast cereal in diamond shapes rather than squares. Now, as was pointed out by somebody who commented on my column on Shreddies, the new Shreddies were just the old Shreddies squares turned on their side. Actually, I kind of got that. What that critic missed was the simplicity and power of turning the old shape on its side. It demonstrates the strength of looking at "same-old" through a fresh lens. This campaign worked because it was unexpected, engaging, fresh and fun. Imagine a cereal commercial that didn't just focus on the same old serving suggestion and how great it was for your kids and grandkids. Not only did this unique campaign push sales, I have heard stories of the limited edition boxes of "new diamond" Shreddies being sold as collector's items on eBay. Wow! What a little divergent thinking can do for a brand.

Seeing a new message in an old brand

Similarly, Nabisco came up with an innovative idea for its 100-year-old Oreo cookie, and turned it into a social media publicity bonanza. They created an ad that showed the cookie's traditionally white filling bearing all the colors of the rainbow, and ran the ad in support of Gay Pride in June 2012. Within 24 hours Nabisco's Facebook page racked up more than 52,000 "shares" and 177,000 "likes" – and nearly 38,000 comments[1]. The reputation and brand of both Nabisco and its parent company, Kraft, were enhanced manifold by this simple idea. Although some thought it would cause a negative backlash, it was a successful, powerful statement of social responsibility that also powered a dramatic surge in brand awareness. One simple idea and a world of new awareness.

Exploring new markets with the same products (or slightly adapted)

Toy giant Lego has launched a "Lego Friends" brand for girls as an add-on and extension of its dominating boy brands like Star Wars Lego and Ninjago. A simple addition that reaches an entirely new market.

---

[1] *Rainbow-colored Oreo, a harbinger of more gay advertising, by Dan Zak, Washington Post, Lifestyle, June 27, 2012*

Tapping into (or teaming up with) new market trends

Hyundai now provides a multimedia tablet as an owner's manual instead of the traditional printed book. What a great way to exemplify innovative thinking and reinforce its brand at a touch point that has remained the same for decades. Now, with this sleeker approach to the die-hard thick and heavy printed manual, customers can actually fit more stuff in the limited glove compartment space. The combining of two disparate ideas into one great innovation.

Bringing together features from existing products or markets to create something new

Big Time Brands, the maker of the SLAP Watch, offers a unique twist on silicone watches with interchangeable faces, bright colours, and one-size-fits-all spring-coil bracelet – all in one affordable item.

Addressing what everyone else has ignored

Dyson Ltd.'s innovations are so obvious and yet, so breakthrough: safe, bladeless fans that move air around a room without the rumbling and rattling of conventional bladed fans. Dyson also uses technology patterned after jet engines to create dual-cyclonic vacuums that suck up more dirt more efficiently, and wall-mounted hand driers that really work.

Dyson is the clear leader in recognizing and addressing age-old customer frustrations that other companies seem to have ignored for decades. In doing so, Dyson has also taught some former market leaders a good lesson in innovation – don't be afraid to make yourself obsolete, or someone else will.

Why were all these products not developed sooner? Did no other company listen to generations of frustrated consumers? Or were the former market leaders simply too afraid to cannibalize existing products and markets by introducing something more innovative?

The innovation continuum

We have demonstrated that innovation can be simple, and that it can drive your business through both process innovation, and product and service innovation. Simple-adaptive is the process that produces a constant incremental string of small wins. But you don't need to settle for just "adapting," because as you move forward new horizons open up, and ever-expanding opportunities will be discovered. That is because innovation is a continuum, from simple-adaptive to focused-disruptive.

> *We are constantly in the innovation game, thinking of things that have yet to be done. Asking, what else would serve our customer's purpose?*
>
> *Isadore Sharp, CEO, Four Seasons Hotels*

Focused-disruptive innovation platform

I start my workshops with examples of "simple" innovations – from Dyson and Apple to Shreddies and Cake Pops – for a good reason. Many people don't see innovation as applying to them. They see it as exclusive to certain industries or functions, such as technology, science or engineering. They say they are "just" in sales or finance or operations, and that innovation is big-idea-centric and belongs in the R&D department or at the annual retreat. Wrong, wrong, wrong! Great business leaders know innovation is not just about big ideas. It's about good ideas. Relevant ideas. And they may relate to any aspect of the business, from how you market the product, to how you sell, administer, account, engineer, design, pick, pack, ship and deliver it.

Great business leaders know innovation is not just about big ideas. It's about good ideas. Relevant ideas. And they may relate to any aspect of the business, from how you market the product, to how you sell, administer, account, engineer, design, pick, pack, ship and deliver it.

Focused-disruptive may describe bigger breakthroughs that manifest themselves in wonderful disruptive change in the market - but high-impact innovation starts with the same tenets as simple-adaptive: A deep understanding of your company and your market, and how you can continually re-engage customers while staying focused on growth *and* cost savings. That said, let's look at the other side of the coin: How innovation can create whole new businesses or divisions of businesses.

Focused-disruptive means that you are still focused on your core business but that each new idea, such as the iPod, or OMI's odor-control products, has the potential to disrupt and open up a whole market. It means that you have a vision and platform for your company that is not defined by the commodity that you make, but by the impact you make on your customers' lives. Let's say that again, because this may be the single most important element in becoming a truly innovative company. *You don't define your business by the commodity you make, but by the impact that you can make on your customers' lives.* Here are a few more examples, big and small.

The first is a company that redefined itself from a manufacturer of hearing aids (a commodity) to a hearing-technology company based on user benefits: amplification of sound and noise reduction. By doing so, they asked themselves where else they could apply their market leadership. Their answer: Bluetooth headsets. They put their hearing aids into a headset and added an inexpensive microphone. Next, they built an upgraded, more rugged model for the military. Who could benefit more from clarity of communication than a soldier in the field? The company focused on what they were best at, and looked for logical next-step adaptations that could open up significant new markets.

Woodbridge Company Ltd.

As I was reading the book *Passion Capital* by Canadian executive Paul Alofs, I came across an account of the late Toronto millionaire Ken Thomson, who expanded his family empire from $500 million to $25 billion by understanding the principles of focus and platform. Alofs notes that the son of newspaper magnate Roy Thomson "concentrated on a narrow range of investments in order to stay focused." Thomson liked to say, 'Don't water the wine.'" Alofs continues, "To see a business in the long term, you first have to define what your business is. Was he selling newspapers? Textbooks? The answer was yes, but what he was actually selling was information and knowledge. Understanding this difference and relentlessly focusing on it, Thomson got into digital publishing early on." (I highly recommend Alofs' book. It's full of great insights on how to leverage energy, intensity, and sustainability to generate superior business results.)

Oprah

Imagine if Oprah Winfrey had thought of herself as "just" a talk-show host? She might still be a local, one-station-wonder. The cornerstone of her appeal and success was her platform of self-empowerment: Recognizing how important it is in an overwhelming world to equip oneself with self-belief and spirit. She innately recognized everyone's inner questioning: Where am I going, and how am I going to get there? Her insights into her target audience's wants and needs allowed her to turn a simple question into a multimedia juggernaut that has touched hundreds of millions of lives. Some people may ask me why Oprah's new OWN network is struggling when it's a natural extension of her work and builds on her proven platform. I suspect it's too much of a good thing! This wasn't a 10% step; an all-Oprah network was

You don't define your business by the commodity you make, but by the impact that you can make on your customers' lives.

a quantum leap, moving from about six hours of programming a day (her show, Dr. Phil. Dr. Oz, etc.) to 24/7. But don't ever discount the power of Oprah's message. I would never bet against Oprah or the power of her platform.

Dove

This well-known brand never defined itself as a bar of soap, but as a "beauty bar." The use of the word "beauty," and later the phrase "Real Beauty," freed the brand developers from the notion of just another commodity (soap); it opened up a new and empowering world of opportunity. Dove took a holistic approach to beauty and more specifically, the idea of finding beauty in yourself, not in the perfect, model-inspired airbrushed glamour that is often served up as false hope and empty motivation. This notion of *real* beauty transcended product thinking, enabling numerous product extensions, breakthrough motivational ad campaigns, and even the launch of Dove Spas, where the customer actually becomes the beauty.

The overriding moral is that innovation is not rocket science. You don't have to try and drop a fragile and highly complex land rover on the surface of Mars – at least not right out of the gate. In fact, "Curiosity" landed on Mars in August 2012 because of more than 43 years of simple-adaptive and focused-disruptive innovation. Landing a man on the moon was one small step along the continuum, and one giant step for innovation. It started in 1961 with a declaration of leadership by President John F. Kennedy. He made the decision to cause a serious disturbance in space travel – to land people on the moon by the end of the decade. That decision led to many small steps – and some failures – but eventually it became a triumphant and focused-disruptive platform of innovation. (Of course, some could say the mission began in 1957 when the Russians caused the first disturbance by launching Sputnik, but the Americans pushed ahead, undeterred. On July 20, 1969, well ahead of the competition, they landed on the moon.) Today, the two former "space race" competitors, the U.S. and Russia, are working more and more together to go beyond what anyone might have imagined. The Americans' focused-disruptive platform, despite major cost cuts, still prevails, and landing mankind on Mars is a whole new opportunity. The lesson: First, decide to do it (we call this leadership). Start with baby steps; aim to go just 240,000 miles. And someday, you will go 34 million miles.

> *We choose to go to the moon. We choose to go to the moon in this decade and do the other things, not because they are easy, but because they are hard, because that goal will serve to organize and measure the best of our energies and skills, because that challenge is one that we are willing to accept, one we are unwilling to postpone, and one which we intend to win, and the others, too.*
>
> President John F. Kennedy, September 12, 1962, at Rice University, Houston, Texas

Opportunities for innovation and growth are right in front of us if we make listening, seeing and innovative thinking part of our daily routine. They are a natural extension of what we are already doing. This idea is reinforced by Malcolm Gladwell in his book *Outliers*. Gladwell draws on research that says it takes around 10,000 hours to become an expert in something new. As we pointed out in our earlier book, *The 90% Rule: What's Your Next Big Opportunity?*, the best new opportunities are in adjacent products and markets where you already know 90% of what you need to succeed. Your company's unique capabilities and experience are the key to determining your next innovation success – because you've already put in those 9,000 hours! It should come as no surprise that companies like Disney, Apple, OMI and Dyson focus on leveraging their inherent expertise and core competencies.

Cause a disturbance

My time spent with entrepreneurs and corporate intrapreneurs has taught me that they all share a desire to create something new. An essential strand in their DNA compels them to disrupt the status quo and cause a disturbance. That's why they do what they do, how they come up with great ideas, fill new needs and shake up their marketplaces. They're natural-born innovators – but sometimes, something happens.

Some entrepreneurs lose that killer instinct as their role evolves from disruptor to operator and manager. They spend more time and energy pushing paper – doing what they *have to do* rather than what they are wired to do. They move too far out of their comfort zone, away from where they create real value, and become encumbered by running the business instead of building it. What comes naturally to them is innovation, and yet those days of leading focused team to challenge long odds end up becoming a historical footnote, with the caption, "The good ol' days."

> ### *To love what you do and feel that it matters – how could anything be more fun?*
>
> *Katharine Graham (1917-2001) Publisher, Washington Post*

In fairness, we must admit that being more focused and innovative can become problematic in *some* corporate environments, where the label "entrepreneur" tends to have a negative, "rogue" connotation. The CEO may prattle on about innovation and profess to want more entrepreneurial thinking, but often this is nothing more than talk. True innovative spirit fails to trickle down because the last thing the hierarchy wants is anyone being disruptive. To be entrepreneurial is to think and work outside the rules and boundaries, and that "just ain't gonna be allowed." At least not until *Titanic* hits the iceberg. The IBM of a couple of decades ago was an example of that thinking – big-blue square pegs in big-blue round holes – until new CEO Lou Gerstner Jr. turned things around. To do that he had to convince long-time IBMers to cut the price of mainframe computers to meet the PC challenge, and to move away from hardware into services (in other words, using their technology edge to solve customers' problems directly). In the 1980s, Apple suffered a similar hardening of the arteries the same fate with John Sculley's "same old, same old" corporate thinking replacing Steve Jobs' entrepreneurial approach. Sculley, a former Pepsi executive, said profits came first, products second. Apple co-founder Jobs thought the exact opposite. In his biography of Jobs, Walter Isaacson writes: "Jobs wanted Apple 'to become a wonderful consumer products company,' Sculley wrote, 'This was a lunatic plan... Apple would never be a consumer products company. We couldn't bend reality to all our dreams of changing the world... High tech could not be designed and sold as a consumer product.'" Of course, under Sculley, the under-visioned Apple went into freefall.

It's not that profits are not important. But they are a result of creating great products that satisfy customers. Without a commitment to market-leading products, companies get stale. When Steve Jobs returned to Apple in 1997, he once again infused the company with innovative thinking. Do you remember Job's famous Apple advertising campaign, "Think Different"? ("Here's to the Crazy Ones! The misfits... the ones who see things differently..."). This was more than an advertising campaign; it was the company's formal restatement of its brand, its mantra. Sure, it was grammatically wrong, but even that was intentional for a company bent on market disruption. With this new brand message, Apple achieved what we all want in our businesses, a seamless melding of simple-adaptive and focused-disruptive innovation. And Jobs didn't just innovate products (iPod) and services (iTunes); he innovated process in every facet of the business so that Apple could create more new innovations than the competition, and deliver them faster to market.

One of the most significant takeaways from Steve Jobs' story is his unfettered instinct for leaping beyond research and what customers thought they wanted, to imagining what products would most delight customers if they could be developed. Plus, Apple never stops adapting its products and re-engaging customers by introducing new and better versions. The innovation continuum is a fully integrated reality at Apple. Its phenomenal sales results ($156 billion in 2012, up nearly 50% in one year) say it all. When innovation, marketing and sales coalesce around the same goals and strategy, the innovation continuum becomes the driving force for growth. Without a doubt, Apple has been the world's most successful turnaround. And innovation was, and still is, the heart and soul of that turnaround.

How did it happen? In the 1990s, Apple Computer was swimming in a sea of red ink, its glory days as a disruptive innovator in the personal computer industry long behind it. Microsoft's Windows programs had appropriated the graphical, easy-to-use operating system that had made Apple's Macintosh so popular among artists, designers and engineers. Microsoft's unmatched distribution power was slowly crushing Apple's innovation edge.

The world will be a better place with Apple in it.

Steve Jobs (upon his return to Apple)

But in January 1997 Apple's creative co-founder, Steve Jobs, returned to the company after a decade away (he returned first as an advisor, and was named CEO again in 2000). While he introduced such radical innovations as the one-piece iMac computer (processor and monitor in one desktop unit!), Apple continued to lose market share. But Jobs had another plan up his sleeve. Apple didn't have to confine its design and usability expertise to the PC market.

Technology was now transforming consumer culture – especially in music, where convergence of computer and communications technology had created a huge market for portable music (and illegal copying of songs over the Internet, through file-sharing sites such as Napster).

In October 2001 Apple introduced the iPod: a gleaming white piece of plastic that could store and replay 1,000 songs. Although not the first MP3 player, the petite but powerful iPod, with its innovative (and intuitive) scroll-wheel interface, was the first to make the category sexy. And Apple's distinctive "ear buds" became a sought-after status symbol.

With its engineering horsepower, Apple regularly turned out innovative new iPod models, beefing up their storage capacity even as the product shrunk to become more convenient and nearly weightless. By 2006, the iPod accounted for nearly half of Apple's revenues.

But Jobs also addressed the problem of music piracy. Using Apple's 75% share in portable music players he introduced the iTunes Store: a centralized, easy-to-use system for managing music that proved so powerful that Jobs was able to force the recording industry to accept his take-it-or-leave-it price of just 99 cents a song. iTunes has now sold more than 16 billion songs.

In 2007, Apple dropped "Computer" from its name, to reflect its broader view. Apple Inc. now boasts that its mission is to "bring the best user experience to its customers through its innovative hardware, software, peripherals, and services." That's no hyperbole. In 2007 Apple's iPhone transformed the market, combining Apple's computer expertise, Internet experience and user knowledge. The iPhone led to a new level of Apple-based innovation, as more than 100,000 software developers, worldwide, created new iPhone applications for downloading through Apple's "App Store." In the fiscal year ended September 2011, iPhone-related products and services generated sales of a whopping $47 billion, or 43% of Apple's total sales of $108 billion.

Apple's stunning success shows how easily a core competency in one industry can be carried into other markets. As the iPod begat the iPhone, the iPhone begat the iPad. That fun and functional tablet computer created another new product category, reaching seniors and children and many other holdouts who had never owned a computer before. The iPad, in just its second year on market, generated $20 billion in sales in fiscal 2011.

Apple has continued to innovate, with iCloud storage and Apple TV. Although Jobs died in October 2011 – generating an outpouring of emotion never seen for any other CEO – the company he built seems likely to continue its winning ways. In 2012 Apple unseated Exxon Mobil as the world's most valuable company with a market capitalization value of more than $600 billion. Also in 2012, Fortune Magazine named Apple the world's most admired company – for the fifth year in a row.

An interesting postscript to Apple's story is the fact that in 2007, one of the leading gurus on innovation said that the iPhone would not be successful. Clayton Christensen, a Harvard professor and author of several books on innovation, basically said that the iPhone was too expensive and that "disruption" tends to come from the bottom up in an industry, not top-down. In hindsight, he got it wrong because the iPhone was not really a phone, but a fun, easy-to-use mini-computer. Coming in at the bottom of the computer industry (not at the "top" of the phone industry), it caused a huge disturbance in the portable computer market. Much cheaper, more portable and more convenient than a laptop, the iPhone caused one of the biggest disturbances in consumer markets in decades. It was a focused-disruptive innovation that continually applies simple-adaptive innovation with every new version and spinoff.

Imagine the disturbance. Imagine the profits. In recent years, pundits have asked whether Microsoft has lost its entrepreneurial way, a decade after Bill Gates handed the reins over to Steve Ballmer, who had been hired as Microsoft's first business manager in 1980. Has the high-tech behemoth rested too long on its Office and Windows laurels, and buried entrepreneurial thinking – and innovation along with it – under a truckload of bureaucratic operating dogma and the obesity of billions in cash? Endless money doesn't guarantee innovation. When one thinks of innovation today, Microsoft is probably not your first thought. Still, the big M has been trying to resuscitate an innovative culture, introducing several significant products to the market in 2012. In an article in the October 2012 issue of *Fast Company*, Austin Carr posited: "Windows 8 aims to change the way we've been interacting with computers for the past three decades. Windows 8 could also transform the nature of the software giant's competition with home-run king Apple, potentially reversing a string of embarrassing defeats, especially in the mobile market. Even more improbably, Microsoft is building this comeback attempt not on its traditional strength – engineering – but on, of all things, design."[2] That's focused-disruptive. Will Microsoft cause a disturbance in the marketplace? Time will tell.

The world of tomorrow belongs to the person who has the vision today.

Robert Schuller

Innovation is rooted in an understanding of entrepreneurial thinking and the belief that great things come from disrupting the status quo and causing a disturbance in the marketplace. But rather than guilting business owners, partners and leaders into generating innovation, I prefer to remind them that their instinct for disruption and discovery is the reason they are executives and entrepreneurs in the first place. It's what got them here. Turning ideas into action made them flourish. I have seen, over and over, where new ideas put the bounce back in a company's step and put more "rev" in their revenue statements. It begins with understanding the two principles I mentioned in Chapter 3: 1) Innovation is easier than you think; and 2) It's about causing a disturbance in markets. Innovation happens along a continuum that becomes a driving force in your business.

To all the entrepreneurs and intrapreneurs chained to their desks and baffled by their own bureaucracy, my suggestion is simple: Offload a bunch of operational responsibilities to someone who loves to load up their left brain, and focus your passion on the next epiphany pinging around in your right brain. Do it. Even if at first an idea doesn't turn into a full-fledged profit center, you will see immediate gains as your

[2] *"Microsoft Wipes The Slate Clean," Fast Company, October 2012, Austin Carr, p. 122*

Rather than guilting business owners, partners and leaders into generating innovation, I prefer to remind them that their instinct for disruption and discovery is the reason they are executives and entrepreneurs in the first place. It's what got them here. Turning ideas into action made them flourish.

people embrace innovation and the discovery process works its way into their daily activities. innovation is contagious; it will infect the people around you. With that spirit in place, innovation will sprout up where you least expect it.

It's time to reassert yourself as your company's Chief Innovation Officer, and inspire your team to start thinking about possibilities, rather than just operating the status quo, punching in and out, and blindly shuffling the deckchairs. The good news is that it's not a big step; you are already 90% of the way there.

Permission to cause a disturbance

"Ordinary people control their brands and their destinies."

Sir Richard Branson

We all know what innovative cultures can do. You've seen companies like Virgin, Google, Apple and Disney thrive and grow under the leadership of original thinkers. You've seen new upstarts such as Under Armour and Spanx shake up the stodgy underwear industry, with the leaders of both companies recently vaulting onto the latest Forbes magazine "Billionaire's List." Their secret ingredients are no secret. They and their teams are driven by entrepreneurial thinking, working in an innovative environment, connected by a process for innovation and allowed – encouraged – to upset the status quo. Go ahead: Slice up those melons, make all right-hand turns, rotate the Shreddie, support gay pride, digitize the owner's manual, and let the marketing, sales engineering and manufacturing people work hand-in-hand, every day, to upgrade company processes, cut costs and provide better service. Just watch what happens.

As a leader, give yourself and your people permission to question the status quo and imagine and explore new ideas. And then decide which ones you want to do. Don't wait. Don't dither. Do it!

A hunch is creativity trying to tell you something.

Frank Capra, American filmmaker

If you dedicate yourself to causing a disturbance you will rediscover your own eureka muscles, release the innovative spirit in your people and lift your business' bottom line. Your people will be more invested in the company and everyone will have more fun. Not bad for something that is easy to do. And you're already 90% of the way toward doing it.

Part

TWO

The 90% Rule® and Defining Your Core Business

No, you don't make tape, you enable people to attach, seal or secure things to each other. Now, how else can you help them do that?

Chapter

6

The 90% Rule®

It's about getting more out of what you already have and do.

Ken Tencer

I didn't write a foreword for this book, but I now say, "Forward." It's a directive and direction — a call to action — for those who want to put more innovation into their business so they can get more growth for a lower financial investment. In a word: leverage. That's the *90% Rule.*

The 90% Rule is the principle underlying the innovation process we've been talking about. It is anchored in the fact that you already know (and have available to you) 90% of what you need to succeed.

At the core of the 90% Rule is entrepreneurial thinking, which stubbornly insists that there is never a shortage of opportunities – only a perceived shortage of resources with which to capitalize on them. This type of thinking contrasts with two common and misdirected practices:

1) Believing they have limited capital available, companies avoid developing the best opportunities because of this perceived lack of resources (time, people, money).

I didn't write a foreword for this book, but I now say, "Forward." It's a directive and direction — a call to action — for those who want to put more innovation into their business so they can get more growth for a lower financial investment. In a word: leverage.

By entrepreneurial thinking, I mean the ability to envision and think about opportunities at many different levels; to see both the big picture and the relevant details; to act on those details in the most innovative way; and to get the most out of limited resources.

2) Companies chase opportunities on merely a tactical basis, rather than strategically, because they have not defined the broader context in which they are making decisions. Thus they miss the easy, adjacent opportunities that don't require complex retooling and re-engineering.

The 90% Rule helps you to successfully overcome these impediments by addressing five fundamentals:

1. Gain maximum leverage with the assets you already have.

2. Understand your core business from a visionary level.

3. Identify and profile your most lucrative target markets.

4. Develop logical, next-step projects that are actionable and measurable – and aligned with your vision, goals and strategy.

5. Make innovation a front-burner issue so that you are always a step ahead of your competitors and the market.

One other plus: The 90% Rule helps to minimize the risks of innovation and maximize your focus on the best opportunities.

> **Entrepreneurs are simply those who understand that there is little difference between obstacle and opportunity, and are able to turn both to their advantage.**
>
> *Victor Kiam, former CEO, Remington Corporation*

Achieving more with less

Let me first explore two examples that represent the antithesis of entrepreneurial and platform-based innovative thinking. For years now I've heard business "news" stories where a CEO announces that his or her company will shed non-core assets and focus on doing what it does best. I ask, "Why did you get away from your core business in the first place?"

Secondly, too often have I seen traditional consultants go into successful, profitable companies and tell them what's wrong with the business, instead of building on what they're doing right. This makes no sense to me, and it's not the way an entrepreneurial mind works.

Entrepreneurs have always fascinated me. I've been one – and studied others – for years in order to better understand how they/we think. The great ones, from Gutenberg and Ford to Branson and Jobs, have a knack for seeing opportunities, big and small, and finding a way to make them happen no matter what the odds. I believe that entrepreneurial thinking is at the root of all successful change and growth. It is the key to innovation. And the good news is that everyone can cultivate their own entrepreneurial mindset. This could help you start a business, grow and evolve that business, as well as accelerate your personal and professional growth.

By entrepreneurial thinking, I mean the ability to envision and think about opportunities at many different levels; to see both the big picture and the relevant details; to act on those details in the most innovative way; and to get the most out of limited resources. It's being creative, innovative and resourceful, and anchoring all that in the power of leverage so as to get the most out of the resources you already have.

The 90% Rule focuses on expanding the individual and collective capacity for entrepreneurial thinking in order to accelerate an organization's growth. *It is an organizing principle designed around a process that cultivates the creative thinking of an organization by connecting it to corporate competencies, company strategy and customer needs – whether spoken or unspoken.*

Our seminars and this book – and all our thinking and action – are inspired by entrepreneurial thinking. It fuels innovation with passion, will and leverage. But great innovators know that thinking alone is not enough; it needs a means to reach its end. You need a process to convert entrepreneurial energies and thinking into actionable, measurable, profitable opportunities.

Three "how-tos"

Your business needs three creative capabilities:

1) How to foster continuous innovation and growth through the doctrine of entrepreneurial thinking— "innovation against all odds." This means leveraging intellectual and customer capital, continually generating ideas and opportunities, and executing it all *without* bundles of additional money.

2) How to develop a disciplined process that builds on and reinforces the best in your organization: people, processes, products and services. This process elevates everything to new levels.

3) How to install and maintain an iterative process for identifying and exploiting innovative opportunities which you are already 90% capable of achieving.

The entrepreneur is the most important player in the building of the global economy. So much so that big companies are decentralizing and reconstituting themselves as networks of entrepreneurs.

John Naisbitt, author, Global Paradox and Megatrends

Six applications of The 90% Rule

Many different types of organizations at different stages can benefit from application of the 90% Rule. Here are six general categories:

1. Focus a new management team (or re-focus an existing one): When an organization needs a cohesive focus around a new management team and/or new initiatives, the 90% Rule uncovers and then shines an unmistakable spotlight on the highest-potential opportunities.

2. Preparing for a funding initiative: When new financing is needed, the 90% Rule can help organizations identify the critical strategic and tactical elements and the requisite leverage that an investor or lender is looking for.

3. Family business in transition: When a family business is transitioning to the next generation, the 90% Rule can help families keep a tight focus on the business goals and overall vision, minimizing distractions and detrimental change.

4. Sales have hit a plateau: In many industries, longstanding brands and organizational cultures have become stagnant, with growth depending on new insights and innovation. By identifying the highest-value growth opportunities, the 90% Rule can lead to high-value returns.

5. More opportunities than resources: As customer demand shifts and new technologies advance, many organizations find they have more opportunities worth pursuing than they have resources to support them. The 90% Rule helps prioritize and manage resource allocation.

6. Shifts in markets and customer needs: When markets are turbulent or customers' needs and wants are constantly changing, the 90% Rule can help you identify and prioritize the best opportunities.

Whether or not your organization's challenges fall neatly into one of the above categories, the 90% Rule is a relevant, easy-to-apply tool for almost every business challenge, because it is powerful process rooted in the fundamental principles of self-knowledge and leverage.

Innovation is the specific instrument of entrepreneurship ... the act that endows resources with new capacity to create wealth.

Peter Drucker

I selected Peter Drucker's quotation because it touches on three important components of the 90% Rule—innovation, entrepreneurship and new capacity. The first two, when combined with a systematic method of prioritizing opportunities, will give you "new capacity to create wealth." The best part is, you just have to cultivate a new way of thinking.

The previously mentioned reference to Malcolm Gladwell's, *Outliers* has a direct relation to the *90% Rule*. In the book, neurologist Daniel Levitin says, "The emerging picture from such studies is that ten thousand hours of practice is required to achieve the level of mastery associated with being a world-class expert – in anything."[3] For me, this learning curve is the recipe for outstanding success in any field. But it's also a reminder of the inherent difficulties in trying to excel at too many things – getting away from your core strengths. It makes no sense for a company to try to become an expert in a whole new field or new market when its next big opportunity probably lies in a simple extension of its current business, brand or mastery. Leveraging the innovation continuum, the 90% Rule is all about figuring out how what you already do well can fit better in current markets or adjacent markets –

[3] *Outliers: The Story of Success by Malcolm Gladwell, page 40*

or in vertical business niches. The fomula is simple: build on your current capital base. Don't over-leverage to get into a new one.

The *90% Rule* is akin to *The Hedgehog and the Fox*[4], an essay that philosopher Isaiah Berlin borrowed from an ancient Greek parable. It's about slow and sure rather than fast and risky—evolution, not revolution. The story divides the world into hedgehogs and foxes. The clever fox knows many things and pursues many things, but the stalwart hedgehog knows one big thing – protection - and pursues it relentlessly. Hedgehogs simplify a complex world into one single powerful organizing idea, a basic principle or concept that unifies and guides everything that the hedgehog knows, thinks and does. The hedgehog epitomizes the fundamental lessons of the *90% Rule: Start with what works. When in doubt, stick with what you know.*

The power of compound interest works. Do the math

There are obviously no guarantees or perfect formulas in business - if there were, the failure rate for new business and products wouldn't be so high. But I have always believed in the potential for steady, controlled growth, and as such, have keyed the *90% Rule* off of the mathematics of compound interest.

What I have always done is define my prior year's sales as my core sales. Set these core sales as 90% of the next year's sales. If this core 90% of my business grows at 5% a year, then that generates 4.5% annual growth. Now, I look to add a new product, service, vertical niche or distribution channel that will expand my sales base by an additional 10%. Result: I target annual growth of a healthy 14.5%. I may not hit this target every year, but the thinking is sound: when you build

[4] *Isaiah Berlin, The Hedgehog and the Fox, an essay, The Study of Mankind, p. 436*

I am a believer in using innovation as leverage for your leverage – operating and financial.

your core and continuously add new ventures around that core, you are providing your business base the opportunity to grow significantly. It's the same principle we rely on to grow our personal investments and retirement plans. And because the 90% Rule focuses on doable incremental growth, it shouldn't overburden your capital base. Instead, it offers you manageable opportunity.

Using innovation as leverage for your leverage

I am a believer in using innovation as leverage for your leverage – operating and financial. This is a cornerstone of the *90% Rule.*

Operating leverage refers to an organization's reliance on, or investment in, fixed assets. We all know it's a challenge to manage overhead costs, and if you have too many fixed assets, you are always scrambling to cover those costs every month. Financial leverage uses debt to fund growth and increase production. But, too many fixed assets (or too much debt) will land you regular calls from a not very happy banker. You need to strike a reasonable balance between leverage and prudence so that when the unexpected happens, you can survive it.

Innovation is a great way to get more out of your assets and drive better returns from your investments because levering, or building on, core competencies is a low-cost way of giving your company a more secure future.

Diamonds are created under pressure

Good leverage makes the most of an organization's most robust current strengths, which is where your principal growth initiatives should focus. Focus on what's right, not what's wrong. Deal from strength, not weakness (i.e. the cost of capital). Growth leverage springs from rethinking and re-understanding the capital investments you have already made, as well as the ways in which your business serves its customers and potential customers (e.g., fixed assets, cash and intellectual capital, as well as customer capital).

We haven't got the money, so we've got to think.
Ernest Rutherford, British physicist

My own businesses are typical examples of adjacent growth through leverage. I have never had the opportunity to start or build a company with an excess of cash. My partners and I have always done it the old–fashioned way – with a bucket, a paddle and a couple of credit cards. In the beginning years, it's like a recession every day. But this is a great way to start because it encourages three behaviors that are requisite to success:

 i) A fundamental understanding of your business.

 ii) Ingenuity, innovation and entrepreneurism.

 iii) Leverage that exploits every advantage you can find.

All of these tactics can be more productive and valuable than cash. I use the metaphor that diamonds are created under pressure.

Don't get me wrong. Cash is a wonderful thing. But, in my experience, good thinking and great leverage in times of low cash will get you more growth than cash will get you in the absence of great thinking. This is why I first defined the *90% Rule* around growing a business from an existing base of expertise, equipment and limited capital. I didn't think of "capital" as simply cash. I knew there was great value in other assets, particularly the non–traditional ones (e.g., people, ideas, time). Because of this we have always asked and continue to ask ourselves: What new product or service can we develop based on what we already have, what we already do, or what we *almost* do?

In my current business, this helped us change from thinking of Spyder Works as a strategy and design firm to one focused on helping businesses reimagine their role in the marketplace. We did what I asked you to do a few chapters ago. We stopped defining ourselves in terms of the services we offered, and focused instead on the customer-centered benefits we create. This simple mind-shift from commodity to platform opened our thinking from providing just one-to-one services to adding one-to-many services, such as innovation seminars, books, and online assets. These new products are all based on the same pool of knowledge (intellectual capital), but we have expanded it and repackaged it to share with a greater community of thinkers. This enabled Spyder Works to grow significantly faster, with minimal financial risk. We found a way to leverage what we already had – both the operating assets that we had invested in and the financial instruments that we had used to fund growth.

Innovation is applied creativity.

Don't reorganize, rethink

I was to learn later in life that we tend to meet any new situation by reorganizing; and a wonderful method it can be for creating the illusion of progress while producing confusion, inefficiency and demoralization.

Gaius Petronius Arbiter, 66 A.D.

The 90% Rule is not about "reorganizing." It is about reseeing, rethinking, redoing. It's looking at strategy and operations through a new set of lenses, and exploiting the opportunities within your reach. It sounds simple, even obvious. But most organizations fail to tap this source of innovation and growth, for several reasons:

- They haven't thought about it (especially from an entrepreneurial perspective).
- They haven't found the time to do it.
- They haven't had a clear understanding of how to do this effectively.
- They do it once in a while, often by accident, but fail to create a process for doing it continuously and strategically.

The Power of the 90% Rule: More with less

Capitalizing on your existing resources simply takes more innovative thinking. With the right customer-focused perspective, you will be surprised how much you can leverage your brand equity, intellectual capital, customer capital, product capital, and physical assets.

Hedgehogs and tortoises

I believe in the principle of hedgehogs and tortoises, in winning the race with methodical innovation, not chasing the next quick fix. I believe in long-term sustainable growth, not short-term performance "hits." I believe in evolution, not revolution. (Revolutions tend to be short-term fixes, and their most common product is counter-revolutions.).

In the race for success, speed is less important than stamina. The sticker outlasts the sprinter.
Bertie Charles Forbes (1880-1954) Founder, Forbes magazine

If you have a sound product and market, you're already 90% of the way to a better future – and moving ahead has a great deal to do with how you view your business.

Chapter

Understand Your Core Business: Then Disrupt the Status Quo

> **Be who you are. Just do more of it more often for more people.**
>
> *Ken Tencer*

Most entrepreneurs start businesses because they see an opportunity to do something better, something different from the competition. They're in business to leverage new ideas to shake up sleepy markets. By definition, the function of an entrepreneur is to disturb the status quo, to blaze a new trail, to make a difference.

> **I'm not an entrepreneur. I like rules too much, and entrepreneurs break rules.**
>
> *Guy Hands, CEO, Terra Firma Capital Partners*

You can't begin to be different if you don't know who you are and what you do best. Many entrepreneurs and business leaders don't take the time to figure out what business they are really in, and what the market really needs; most work with a lot of guessing and assuming. Consequently, most businesses get stuck in doing and running *what already is*

You can't begin to be different if you don't know who you are and what you do best. Many entrepreneurs and business leaders don't take the time to figure out what business they are really in, and what the market really needs; most work with a lot of guessing and assuming.

instead of thinking, understanding and innovating *what could be*. For instance, someone, somewhere once asked: Can a gas station sell more than gas? Is a corner store in the business of selling milk, snacks, cigarettes - or does it provide a web of convenience for busy customers? And in today's go-go world, how important is time?

Innovative thinking begins by questioning the status quo. In the case of selling more than gas and sundries, it's hard to differentiate commodity products – but you can deliver a difference when it comes to time and convenience. That's why we have seen what used to be just gas stations turned into multipurpose convenience centers selling fresh coffee and hot snacks, complete with drive-thrus, ATMs, lotto centers, grocery sections and ever-broadening product selections. This evolution is even evident in the branding, with new logos such as ExxonMobil's "On the Run" stations looking to create brand-equity in the corner-store sector. This type of adjacent thinking isn't new: in 1927 John Jefferson Green, who operated a few ice-houses, thought customers might find it convenient if he leveraged the temperature in his facilities by also selling products, such as milk and butter, that benefit from adjacency to ice. Two decades later, the name of his few small stores was changed to brand the convenience he had created. Today, 7-Eleven has 46,000 outlets; it's the largest convenience store network in the world.

If you don't understand what your customers value, and how your roots connect to their needs, then it will be difficult for you to know which assets and ideas will get your organization where you want to go. The good news is that there are countless examples of companies – big and small, famous and infamous – that have succeeded by figuring out what business they are *really* in. Have you figured it out?

If you don't understand what your customers value, and how your roots connect to their needs, then it will be difficult for you to know which assets and ideas will get your organization where you want to go.

*"Would you tell me please, which way I ought
to go from here?"*
*"That depends a good deal on where you want
to go."*
"I don't much care where."
"Then it doesn't matter which way you go."

Through the Looking Glass by Lewis Carroll

True to your core

Disney has always been different – a step above and a step ahead of all the wannabe-Disney film studios and theme parks, and yet, always true to its core business. Disney executives don't lose sight of the power of leveraging what they are already good at. They know they are selling a dream, and the dream is rooted in the original entrepreneurial spirit of Walt Disney himself. He made sure the company's brain trust always remembered who they were and what they were good at, and that they never veered too far from improving and expanding on what they did best. "Walt's way" was anchored in four steps: "Dream, Believe, Dare, Do."[5] Disney is built on a platform of innovation that allows the company to constantly move between simple-adaptive and focus-disruptive.

We can learn from them all. From Apple and Disney to 7-Eleven and OMI, we see that growth is fueled by entrepreneurial thinking, which begets innovative thinking, which *causes a disturbance* that is rooted in an organization's core strength. It's not just the big guys; thousands of small and medium-size companies shake up their marketplaces every day.

**When you see a successful business, someone
once made a courageous decision.**

Peter Drucker

---

[5] *The Disney Way, Capodagli and Jackson, p. xi*

G Adventures

Bruce Poon Tip started his own adventure-travel company, Toronto-based G Adventures, as a way of exploring his personal values. He had traveled through Thailand like a native, riding broken-down buses, staying in small, family-run hotels and eating local foods. Pitying the Western tourists with their air-conditioned motor coaches, he decided to launch his own company to help venturesome Westerners access authentic travel and cultural experiences through small-group trips to offbeat destinations around the world.

Today, G Adventures is the world's largest adventure-travel firm with sales of more than $100 million, 100,000 customers per year, and tours on all seven continents. Now respected as an international expert on eco-tourism, Poon Tip has never sacrificed his personal values for growth. But he has learned to think big and embrace multiple target markets.

He began by selling tours to Thailand and the ruins of Machu Picchu in Peru and now sells more than 1,000 different tours. He realized early on that his company had to appeal to more than just backpackers even though his first brochure warned, "If you'd like all the comforts of home, we suggest you stay home."

Poon Tip's true target: anyone looking for an alternative to conventional tourism and three-star beach resorts. Today he targets high-income singles, families, photography buffs, gourmets, affluent retirees and other niche groups through a range of specialty tours – including a $13,000 voyage to Antarctica by icebreaker.

G Adventures grew by realizing that the product it's selling is not simply travel but *experience*. Satisfied customers sign up for trips year after year because they trust the company to connect them to unique new experiences – adventure in the company of like-minded travelers.

To reach this independent-minded market, G Adventures has pioneered new marketing techniques: abolishing "single supplements," conducting traveling slide shows to entice prospects and opening brick-and-mortar stores in New York, Toronto, Vancouver and Melbourne. All the while, the rest of the travel industry was focusing on the internet. G Adventures produces its own television shows and online videos and provides an online traveler's forum moderated by satisfied customers, not the company's staff. They have even created their own foundation, Planeterra, to build client relationships and "give back" to the communities G Adventures' travelers visit.

With his company growing 30% a year, Poon Tip admits he is following no road map but instinct. "There's no precedent for a company of our size in this industry," he says. For his next act, he's considering expanding into book publishing, restaurants and hotels. But he has no interest in accepting the many offers he's received to sell his company. "I'm working hard, but I'm having more fun than ever."

G Adventures stuck to its original innovative platform and core capabilities and with ever more simple-adaptive and focused-disruptive innovation, it leveraged its strengths into a global enterprise. Unfortunately, for every story like this one there are too many of the other type: companies that wander away from their core business strengths, for any number of reasons. Two of the more common problems are that these companies either lose sight of what their core business is, or they simply ignore it. Either way, it's rarely a happy ending. Most of the companies I have dealt with over the years fall into the first category. Also, these companies are usually mired in operational pressures and are busy being busy. The

To begin the process of leveraging innovation, the first thing you have to do is take a different view of who you are and how you got to where you are today. This is where the future begins.

pervasive thinking is either, "We haven't got time," or "It's the way we've always done it." They run the business – often the business runs them – by incessantly focusing on sales and marketing and "counting beans." They never find the time to start the real engine of growth, innovation. They think: If we just work harder, do more of what we're doing, and keep scrambling, we'll get there.

> **If the only tool you have is a hammer, after a while everything begins to look like a nail.**
> *Abraham Maslow (1908-1970), American psychologist*

To begin the process of leveraging innovation, the first thing you have to do is take a different view of who you are and how you got to where you are today. This is where the future begins.

Chapter 8

Your Core Business Through a Different Lens

To see things differently, open your eyes and your mind.

John Paulo Cardoso

Let me relate a story originally told by Edward de Bono, a renowned leader in creative thinking and the originator of the term "lateral thinking." This story goes directly to the point of seeing things differently in order to leverage unseen value. My bet is that the Tommy in this story will grow up to be an entrepreneur.

It's all in how you look at it

Tommy is five years old. Typically, he's in constant pursuit of his nine-year-old brother John. And John, like most older brothers, is always picking on Tommy. One day, John and two of his buddies are hanging out in his room when Tommy comes wandering by. John says to his buddies, "Hey guys, wanna get a laugh? Watch this." His friends eagerly gather around. "Tommy, come here."

Pleased with the invitation, Tommy comes into the room, breaks into a big grin and looks up with anticipation. John sits down on the edge of the bed and holds out his hands, palms up. In his right hand is a dime and in his left a nickel. He glances back at his buddies and whispers, "Watch how stupid Tommy is." Turning, he flashes a know-it-all grin at his brother's innocent face. "Hey Tommy, which one of these coins do you want, the big one or the small one?" Tommy's eyes ponder his choices for just a moment. "This one.'" The little guy shoots out his hand, grabs the nickel, jams it in his pocket, and leaves the room.

John triumphantly closes his hand on the dime, breaks into a smug smile, and turns for approval from his buddies. The boys are in stitches. John stops chuckling long enough to say, "Is that stupid or what? He falls for it every time."

The laughter is cut short as a large shadow fills the doorway. It's John's father. "John, your brother is not stupid, and I don't want you playing that trick on him again. Do you hear me?" He gets a guilty reply. "Yeah, okay. We're just playing, Dad. Tommy doesn't care. He likes it." His father interjects sternly, "Well, I'll have no more of it and I'll speak to Tommy, too." He turns and heads for Tommy's room. "Hey Tommy. How you doing?" "Hi Dad." Tommy is sitting in the middle of the floor surrounded by Lego blocks.

"Tommy, I want to explain something to you." Lowering himself onto the floor, he leans back against the end of the bed. Then he spends the next five minutes putting the value of nickels and dimes into context for his son. Using pennies, nickels, dimes and quarters, he shows his son that the size of the coin does not always represent the value of the coin. Throughout the chat, Tommy listens carefully and nods his head. "So, do you see the difference between a nickel and a dime?" asks his father. "Yeah. A nickel is 5 pennies and a dime is 10 pennies," he answers proudly. "Good," says his father. "So the next time John asks you to pick a coin, which one are you going to pick?" Tommy hesitates. and then says, "The nickel."

Exasperation flushes his father's face. "No, Tommy, not the nickel, the dime. It's worth twice as much." Tommy sheepishly reaches under his bed for an old sock, drags it out and turns it upside down. Dozens of nickels fall out of the sock. "Yeah, but if I take the dime John will stop playing the game ... and look how many nickels I've got from him!"

Tommy's audacity never fails to amaze me.

Tommy's father

Tommy understands leverage

New ideas flourish when we change the way we look at things. Tommy saw the obvious in a situation where the "right" answer was actually wrong. John didn't see it, even though it was right in front of him. He never asked the simple question why. Why does Tommy keep coming back? How many nickels is this costing me? Whether you're playing for nickels or millions, seeing things differently can turn the not-so-obvious into the innovative – and nickels into a pile of cash flow.

The *90% Rule* is built on the premise of innovation: See differently. Think differently. Do differently. Earlier, I suggested a simple way to get started at exploring more innovation. Now I want to go deeper into how to develop and integrate an innovative process into your business.

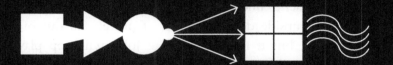

This little
pictogram
will change
how you
view your
business.

The process: Six fundamental steps

This pictogram depicts a new landscape: a place and process from which you can begin to see, think and do differently.

The icons in the pictogram illustrate a six-step process that represents a continuous loop that will trigger new ideas, open up new opportunities and generate new growth. It will identify, rank and map opportunities in markets based on products and services that you are already 90% capable of providing.

This model is designed for businesses and not-for-profit organizations that want a systematic and manageable process. Implementation of the model requires two perspectives:

i) Inside: Knowledge, insight and new thinking,

ii) Outside: Knowledge, objectivity, entrepreneurial thinking and a process that aligns it all.

Managed effectively, the process will turn the little pictogram into a whole new way of doing business.

Step One:

Engaging customer emotion, not numbers.

Step Two:

Exploring what you can be, not just what you are.

Step Three:

Building a relevant brand rooted in customer-centric thinking.

Step Four:

Identifying and ranking your best opportunities based on criteria that objectively assess them.

Step Five:

Building a plan assisted by an opportunity matrix to determine the human and financial resources required for moving ahead.

Step Six:

"Speaking" clearly to all your audiences.

A few of the outcomes

Success accrues to companies that install this integrated process. It's the *90% Rule* in action. The benefits for the companies that do this are clear and tangible. For example:

- You clearly define what business you are in, from a customer viewpoint – including a well articulated vision and mission for your company.
- You establish the right context for strategic decision-making.
- You redefine your target markets and develop a strong position relative to your competition.
- You define and assess a series of actionable and measurable opportunities.
- You identify your communication goals and message to ensure that you are using the most relevant communication tools, always speaking clearly and consistently, and building your brand.
- You install a systematic process that continually supports innovative, long-term growth.
- You consistently align action with strategy.
- You continually innovate and uncover new opportunities.
- You get innovation on the front burner and turn ideas into action on a regular basis.
- You continually leverage your resources.

I know this seems like a lot to do – and promise. But the truth is, once you've institutionalized the process, innovative thinking will become as natural as getting out of bed. Identifying new opportunities, assessing them and getting them onto an action track will become second nature for your people. So as the song goes, "Take time to make time ..."

Some lucky companies have turning points in their history – a time when they pivot the entire company to solve the toughest problems in their market. Achieving this and finding your innovation "sweet spot" isn't easy, and some companies have to take several cracks at it.

San Antonio, Texas, entrepreneur Richard Yoo started Cymitar Network Systems, an internet service provider, in his garage. But as internet access became a commodity, Cymitar quickly refocused on a more creative business, developing internet applications. But it turned out that what Cymitar's customers really needed was someone to manage the technical aspects of their websites. So in 1998, Yoo and his partners pivoted again, founding Rackspace Hosting to assist companies that didn't want to buy and maintain their own web technology.

Rackspace prospered for a time, winning backing from some of Silicon Valley's top venture capitalists. But by 2001, the company was burning cash in the midst of the industry-wide tech meltdown. Rackspace needed to be something more than just another provider of hosting services. But what? That's where they discovered that innovation isn't just about products. It can also be about the service you provide and the culture you create.

Some competitors cut costs and lowered their prices to attract attention or developed new services to bombard their clients with. Rackspace chose a more customer-friendly approach. It decided to offer industry-leading service, realizing that a technical glitch that knocks a website out of commission for even a few hours can cost its owners serious money – as well as frustrate users and possibly drive them away.

"Fanatical Support" became Rackspace's mission – and it remains so today. Much more than a slogan, Fanatical Support became the core of the company's strategy. Most competitors think of themselves as technology companies with an element of service; Rackspace is a service company that happens to be in technology. Its employees are expected to exceed client expectations every day – and have fun doing it. An example: one dedicated "Racker" (the company's name for its employees) was working the phone late one afternoon to solve a customer's problem in another city when she heard one client complain he was hungry. So she ordered them a pizza.

"Fanatical Support" is more than a promise to clients. It's also a blueprint for building the company. Today, more than two-thirds of Rackspace employees are directly customer-facing. Rackspace looks for staff who genuinely enjoy helping others. In return, its employees enjoy a laid-back, flipflop-wearing atmosphere where personality and creativity are encouraged. The company values include: customer experiences that create an emotional attachment; results first, with substance over flash; passion for their work; full disclosure and transparency; and treating fellow Rackers like friends and family. The company's unique culture is key, says CEO Lanham Napier. "Culture is the match that we throw on the gasoline to ignite the Fanatical Support fire."

Rackspace set out to become an employer of choice – and it has been named one of America's 100 Best Companies to Work For in four of the past five years. The UK's Financial Times has named Rackspace to its own list of "Great Places to Work," seven years in a row.

But the acid test of "fanatical support" is customer opinion and behavior. That's why Rackspace is obsessive about monitoring its "Net Promoter Score" – a measure of customer satisfaction created by consultant Fred Reichheld, author of several books on customer loyalty, including

The Ultimate Question. (The ultimate question in business, says Reichheld, is: "Would your customers recommend your products and services to a friend?") Ask your customers to score their willingness on a scale of zero to 10, and your Net Promoter Score will be the percentage of "promoters" in the group (rating you at 9 or 10 out of 10) minus the percentage of "detractors" (those who rate you between zero and 5).

Napier says the NPS is the first metric he looks at every day. "It's an easy, unifying, one number... that lets me know where we stand with the customer," he says. In fact, he says the company's goal is to create customers who are promoters. "Promoters recommend us to their friends, becoming an extension of our sales force. Customers who are promoters are also more profitable, staying with us longer and buying more of our services." Indeed, Rackspace is such a Net Promoter fan that it invited Reichheld to join its board of directors.

The payoff: Rackspace enjoys consistently high NP scores, and the lowest customer-churn rate in its industry. The company's client list (more than 170,000 companies in 120 countries) now includes 60% of the Fortune 500, and 2011 annual revenues passed $1 billion for the first time.

Service innovations can determine a company's future as certainly as product or service innovation. Customer-centric Rackspace is now pinning its future on "cloud" services (in which users access their data and computing power through remote third-party servers). It's a natural move for a hosting company, but Rackspace is pursuing a tack inspired by its commitment to Fanatical Support. Through an innovative partnership with NASA (the National Aeronautics and Space Administration), Rackspace developed a new open-source cloud-computing standard, OpenStack.

Other Cloud suppliers, such as industry giant Amazon, employ "closed" proprietary systems that are incompatible with other services – making captives of their customers. OpenStack is community-driven, which means any organization can help build the system, and clients can easily shift their business between suppliers while keeping their data in-house. Companies backing OpenStack now include Cisco, Dell, Microsoft and HP. Having demonstrated its client commitment in web hosting, Rackspace is clearly looking forward to the competition. As Napier said in a recent blogpost: "We're putting our customers in the driver's seat and empowering them to pack up and move if we're not serving them correctly."

Innovation comes from seeing your business differently and doing your planning based on that new perspective. But planning and time are in constant conflict because neither the business nor the world stops for them. And planning shouldn't stop every time the business or the world changes. It's a Catch-22. That's why you need a consistent process that continuously turns changing circumstances into new innovations and creates innovations that change the circumstances. Installing this process marshals the collective thinking of the business, which is central to growth. Effective planning comes from in-depth thinking. In-depth thinking comes from having time to think. And having time to think comes from having a process that ensures it.

Chapter **9**

Getting Innovative Thinking on the Front Burner

Process, process process ...

Ken Tencer

Problem: Time. Need: Discipline. Solution: Process

Discipline is at the core of the time problem. It's not simply about making extra time; it's about building a fluid process that makes innovative thinking as natural as anything else in business, such as sales, marketing, manufacturing and accounting.

At first this might seem at odds with the way things are – it is – but it can become natural – the way things *should* be. When you create time to consider problems and opportunities and options, you have a much better chance of converting ideas into new solutions. Then day-to-day innovation – by everyone in the organization, from top to bottom – aligns with corporate goals and strategy. The main time issue is about taking the time to build and install the right process. When you do, the return on time (ROT) is significant, the change tangible and the growth measurable.

It's not simply about making extra time; it's about building a fluid process that makes innovative thinking as natural as anything else in business, such as sales, marketing, manufacturing and accounting.

Thinking alone is not enough

We all spend a great deal of time thinking about opportunities, but the issue is the right thinking at the right time with the right application. And the right outcomes.

New thoughts often pop up while we're madly scrambling to complete the next project. They are often good ideas but they seldom get implemented. Even when they do, it's usually too late, because we have gotten sidetracked selling, fixing, reworking, re-estimating … something else. It's about getting thinking in sync with doing. Thinking alone, no matter how innovative, achieves nothing until the ideas are properly considered and turned into action that generates profitable sales and growth.

> ### *Innovation typically occurs at the interface of multiple disciplines.*
>
> *Kenichi Ohmae, author*
> *The Myth & Reality of the Japanese Corporation*

Balance – an elusive goal

The conflict between time and *time to think* always brings us to the eternal balancing act in business, balancing the short and long-term needs of the organization.

It's the old story about the shoemaker whose children went barefoot because he was so busy making shoes for others. We all live that story. Everything seems to be on the front burner – more shoes, more shoes, more shoes … except shoes for our future. Our children's shoes.

In many businesses, front-burner issues eat up the vast majority of time and energy; consequently, time is consumed doing what *has to* be done, not invested in thinking about what *could* be done. Two things always seem to get in the way:

It's the old story about the shoemaker whose children went barefoot because he was so busy making shoes for others. We all live that story. Everything seems to be on the front burner – more shoes, more shoes, more shoes … except shoes for our future. Our children's shoes.

- Ongoing daily pressures of meeting various performance metrics — everything from tracking sales and ensuring deliveries to paring costs and generating profits.

- Things that pop up unexpectedly and "must" be dealt with immediately.

The only thing faster than the speed of change is the speed of thought.

D.H. Hughes, co-author Thoughtware

Experts have known, talked and written about innovation for decades and yet, most companies still struggle with how to catalyze more innovation. Not in the R&D department — many are good there (3M and Corning are two of the best) — but in day-to-day operations. Especially in small and medium size enterprises, where innovation is an unfortunate afterthought or a lucky happenstance, if at all.

Part of 21st century reality is that most companies no longer have the time to "think about" and "sleep on" ideas before making a decision. The future is now. Technology has accelerated the rate of change to the point that it is nearly impossible to keep up. When it comes to the medium- and long-term decisions, many companies simply can't make the best decisions because they've had no time to think about the future before it's on the doorstep. As a result, many decisions are made out of desperation, out of context, and out of touch with market reality. Today, your business is more complex than ever, and under more pressure. It faces shorter timelines and shrinking product life cycles. Today, most everything is "front burner." The key to success is getting innovation there, too.

The easiest way to predict the future is to invent it.

Anonymous (Xerox Research Center)

The 90% Rule applied to innovation and turnarounds

To address the challenges of time, discipline and process, I like to use the example of the gargantuan task of the strategic turnaround. The turnaround requires an extraordinary day-to-day commitment to analysis, questioning, reflection and change. Today, in many ways, the turnaround's lessons reflect and can be applied to the enormous daily pressures that all businesses face. The pressures to address consumer demands, market change and the incessant pressure to innovate, continuously.

The main reason companies fail is lack of focus. They start off doing one thing well and then get attracted to – distracted by – other opportunities. Some may be successful, others not. But all of them distract the owners/management from what they set out to do. And as you know, a lot of times these shiny new opportunities are well removed from your original roots, so there is too little synergy with your established operations and too much to learn. This is where most companies find themselves when in need of a turnaround.

The best turnarounds usually begin with a strategic review that asks: What are our strengths? What do we do best? Where are we losing money? What operations are most profitable? Where can we grow? You can fill in the rest; you know the routine. You might want to consider some of the specific actions that go into a turnaround. Stop doing the same old things, because the definition of insanity is trying to get different results by doing the same thing. And certainly, it starts with firing employees (let's call a spade a spade) who aren't contributing value or lack passion for their job. As soon as you get rid of the complacent and the complainers, your company has a chance to get healthier. But successful turnarounds go well beyond cutting people. Here are a few key elements:

- You need a real "change champion" to manage the turnaround. Someone who owes nothing to the old, failed way of doing things. Someone who is prepared to listen carefully, consider many new ideas and then act ruthlessly when necessary. Their job is to stop the bleeding and get the company moving in the right direction. This is usually a hard job for the original owner/manager to do, but if he or she is determined to do it, it requires hard-headedness and a formal process — designed on the principles of the 90% Rule

- Focus is key. Trimming marginal operations is imperative, as Steve Jobs did when he returned to Apple and cancelled 90% of its product lines in order to focus on only the best and biggest opportunities. A common mistake is to not pull the plug on all non-core activities.

- Reviewing prices and margins is an important step. Many companies are afraid to change prices or set minimum margin or contribution requirements for fear of losing customers, but it's the best way to figure out who your 'best' customers really are and "clean out" the unprofitable ones. The companies I know that have done this all wish they had done it sooner. And every penny of these increases goes directly to the bottom line.

- Refocus on the customer: What do your customers want and need? What are their biggest "pain points," and how can you solve them? Get out and talk to the customers — lots and lots of them (it's a shame so many companies wait until they're in trouble to do this).

Once you have identified new ideas, opportunities and solutions, let the customers know the direction that you plan to take the company.

- Keep employees well informed of the company's plans and decisions, because in the absence of facts, fear can foster confusion and negativity. A common mistake is to not keep employees informed and involved.

- Paint a simple picture of what you're trying to do and the process you are following, and share this vision with everyone (customers, employees, suppliers, investors, bankers, etc.). You want people to know that there is a better future ahead and that their sacrifice, hard work and co-operation will not be in vain. Make sure there is a specific reward at the end, whether it's increased job security, bonuses, profit-sharing or a blowout party to end all parties.

Some turnarounds may require more steps, but you can see how the application of these principles of the 90% Rule begin to provide a consistent, systematic front-burner process for changing the organization, whether you need a major turnaround or simply new opportunities for growth. Either way, change must start with a new attitude and a shot of audacity.

Chapter 10

Getting Thinking to Work

You didn't get here, and you can't get there, by sitting on your status quo with the same thinking, perspective and attitude.

Ken Tencer

I remember the meeting well. I was sitting with a potential client. She was a bright, articulate entrepreneur, and she had created a good product that was just beginning to build traction in the marketplace. She was talking to a number of people to see what might be the "easiest" way to take the company to the next level. There were a number of options open to her. The first was to raise capital and open her own plant, but she did not want the financial risk. The second was to contract a plant overseas to manufacture the product for her. She pointed out that this would entail a lot of due diligence, travel and personal time spent overseeing quality control in another country. She did not want to spend that much time abroad. So she asked me, "What do you think I should do?"

I thought about it for a nanosecond. As hard as I searched my instincts and experience, I could come up with just one answer: "Go to bed and get a good night's sleep. When you wake up, go find a job."

As hard as I searched my instincts and experience, I could come up with just one answer: "Go to bed and get a good night's sleep. When you wake up, go find a job."

It's attitude

On the surface, this may seem glib, even rude. But it really isn't. Business is all about attitude and will, the things that drive us to make a difference, in all facets of our lives. The truth is — any entrepreneur or intrapreneur knows it well — that building a business (yours or someone else's) means sacrifice, risk and uncertainty. If you find the inconvenience of travel or fear of risk a negative factor, then what are you doing in business? Because where I come from, success comes from the heart, the attitude and the will you bring to every problem, every day. If it isn't there, you might as well stay in bed.

> ### *One person with a belief is worth ninety-nine with just an interest.*
>
> *John Stuart Mills (1806-1873) British philosopher*

Montreal entrepreneur Charles Sirois, the chairman of the Canadian Imperial Bank of Commerce, makes for an atypical banker. He has started more than 20 businesses. He calls entrepreneurship "an attitude where you are ready to live with a certain amount of risk ... so that you can face adversity and grow."[6]

Having built a manufacturing firm, I know the risk inherent in securing capital to finance operations, inventory and equipment. Life on the edge isn't for everyone. But it has given me the hands-on understanding needed to find the maximum leverage in what I already have. The key is to know yourself. And also to know your tolerance level for risk, uncertainty and sacrifice, because they're all part of the entrepreneurial equation. Your capacity to balance them and transform them into success gets you out of bed every morning. And you chart your long-term path and choose your everyday actions accordingly. Of course, you don't have to be running your

[6] *Globe and Mail, April 27, 2009*

own business to understand this. Many corporate executives make decisions and take risks that have real consequences to their organizations' growth – and their own future – so the same entrepreneurial thinking is required.

It's audacity

As mentioned earlier, I believe audacity is your best friend. At its core, it provides a powerful combination of self-reliance and independence. Many, if not most, history-changing entrepreneurs have had a large dose of audacity: Johannes Gutenberg, Alexander Graham Bell, Thomas Edison, Henry Ford, Bill Gates (a Harvard dropout), Steve Jobs (another dropout), Jeff Bezos (for years the so-called experts said Amazon was not viable), Sir Richard Branson (talk about daring!) and T. Boone Pickens (from oil to wind energy), to name a few. And, of course, tremendous change has always been delivered by tens of thousands of lesser-known names who have had the audacity to go where others would not.

> *The only way to discover the limits of the possible is to go beyond them into the impossible.*
>
> *Sir Arthur C. Clarke (1917-2008)*
> *British author, inventor, futurist*

This book is not about being an entrepreneur; it's about thinking innovatively – like an entrepreneur – and generating a collective mindset in your organization that understands how to leverage your current assets.

For you and most people in your organization, there are a few entrepreneurial characteristics to look for:

- If you don't believe in yourself and your ideas, you can be sure nobody else will.

- If you don't have passion for your business, it won't come from anybody else.
- If it was supposed to be easy, everybody would be doing it.
- The problems you face are not there to stop you from succeeding, but to stop others from going where you go.
- If there are but a few words to live by, let them be audacity, vision, belief, persistence, will and innovation.

It's not a secret club

I can't tell you how often I've heard people ask, "What is the key to being a successful entrepreneur (or intrapreneur)?" It's as if they believe there is a secret handshake they can learn to become a part of some exclusive entrepreneurs' club. I don't know of any such secret. And from my work with countless entrepreneurs from many different countries, if any of them knew of a secret formula or an off-the-shelf recipe, they didn't share it with me. As I have discovered, success is much more than some manufactured methodology.

I had an interesting experience at a marketing roundtable I was leading for a fast-growing manufacturer of branded and private label products. The founder and CEO was in the session, along with members of the management and sales teams. One of the problems raised by management was that their entrepreneur boss did not share enough of his ideas in advance. He consistently held his cards close to his chest. This made it difficult for managers to make day-to-day, tactical decisions that would support the firm's long-term strategic direction. The owner's surprising and candid response resonated with me immediately. And it still does to this day.

He said, "I don't always share my ideas with everyone because in the past, when I have, there was too much negative reaction and people saying why the idea wouldn't succeed." He found these responses to be demotivating, a deterrent to further action. He added, "And they were usually dead wrong." This from a man who had successfully built and sold one business and was building another that was on a fast track to surpass $100 million in annual revenues. I think most people who understand the underpinnings of entrepreneurial thinking can share his sentiment. I can't think of one successful entrepreneur I have met who doesn't know that negative "can't-do" thinking kills ideas, especially coming from the bottom up. Entrepreneurs can't succeed without an unwavering commitment to their ideas and beliefs. To them, the question isn't "if," but "how". This particular CEO could not get his people to leverage his innovative thinking. His goal, and the reason for engaging our firm, was to help ignite a little more blue-sky, innovative thinking in his team.

Whether you think you can or you can't, you are probably right.

Henry Ford II (1917-1987)
Chairman, Ford Motor Company

There are endless examples of the entrepreneurial spirit driving innovation over other people's objections. I'm sure a couple of guys building the first, user-friendly personal computer in their garage must have had a few naysayers. In 1983, when Steve Jobs talked of his vision for personal computing, he had little outside support. But then, it's human nature to understate potential opportunities. Consider Bill Gates, who said of computer memory in the early eighties, "I think 640k ought to be enough for anyone." Ken Olsen, chairman of Digital Equipment Corporation, in 1977 infamously quipped, "There is no reason for any individual to have a computer in his home." When FedEx's Fred Smith

"I don't always share my ideas with everyone because in the past, when I have, there was too much negative reaction and people saying why the idea wouldn't succeed." He found these responses to be demotivating, a deterrent to further action. He added, "And they were usually dead wrong."

came up with his next-day courier concept, it was summarily panned. So was Jeff Bezos, with his idea for Amazon.

Yeahbut

I've heard a lot of "yeahbuts" as I've listened in the boardrooms, cubicles and halls of business, and none expressed with greater certainty than when a client or prospective client says, "Yeahbut, our business is different." Of course there are differences between individual companies and industries, but in the fundamental principles and processes that I'm talking about, there is little to no difference in their applicability to businesses of all sizes, shapes, colors and functions. Leverage is leverage, finance is finance, marketing is marketing, selling is selling and innovation is innovation. And they all come together when you create a common context for strategic decision-making. What is essential is discovering, defining and building a process within that context. This is where the 90% meets the next 10%. This is where the old view and the yeahbuts transform into a new attitude and new growth.

Rethink to reunderstand and to reinvent

We are all creatures of habit, and the way we think might be the most ingrained habit known to humankind. The famous saying of 16th century philosopher René Descartes, "I think; therefore I am," might be more relevant in our application, if it was, "I think; therefore I can." If we are to change behavior (the doing), we must change the thinking, and if we are to change the thinking, we must have a disciplined approach – a process – that helps us truly see "what is," perceive "what could be," and discover how to achieve it. The process becomes the intrinsic navigator, the gyroscope and the GPS for the way we think and do things.

Obviously, we all spend a lot of time thinking and doing but developing new growth opportunities requires doing things differently. It's not easy. But in our business we make no apologies for having the audacity to push people to change the way they think. And our clients have never asked for one.

There is nothing man won't do to avoid the difficult task of thinking.

Thomas Edison (1847-1931)

Unfortunately, no matter how much or how creatively you think, there is no way to know if what you are planning to do is going to work. That's the entrepreneurial risk every business has to live with. We're not talking about "winging it," we're talking about bringing together thinking and action with a methodology that mitigates risk by moving along a continuum that is systematically in tune with your vision, goals, strategy and customer needs.

There is no shortage of creative people in business. The shortage is of innovators. All too often people believe that creativity alone leads to innovation. It doesn't.

Theodore Levitt (1925-2006)
American economist, Harvard Business School

Trust the process

In this age of expectations over effort, quick fixes over deliberation, and activity over thought, it's a waste of time looking for some mythical panacea or the next revolution. But if you're looking for sustainable change and evolutionary growth, then the 90% Rule gives you a process that marshals thinking and action into sustained growth.

If you have a thought about a new direction or opportunity your business should consider, then you need to find a way to explore it, acid-test it and create go/no go decisions. You need to be able to act in real-time and measure it. At the same time, you need to keep the operational engine oiled and running, balance front-burner issues and continually innovate. Whew! It might not always be "easy," but I assure you it is all straightforward when you have the right process in place. Following a proven framework allows you to deal with everything on a continuous basis, and it gives you more than a fighting chance to grow.

So let's start *doing*. Bring some audacity and a few problems that need fixing, and let's explore how you can turn your organization into an innovation-driven business that will change the lives of your customers – and probably your own life, too.

Part
Three

Working Through The *90% Rule*

Finding opportunities in all the right places.

Preface

*Good planning is as natural to the process of
success as its absence is to the process of failure.*

Robin Sieger, author, Natural Born Winners

I have always liked the saying, "The best place from which
to understand that the earth is round is from the moon."
The same counterintuitive insight is found in the 90% Rule.
To best understand the pragmatic steps required to achieve
your greater vision, you need to view things from a higher,
broader place. If you really want to explore and uncover the
best opportunities, it is important to first look across the entire
spectrum, considering not just what you see today but looking
at where you're going and what you imagine the future to
be. This process lets you move from the big picture to well-
defined, specific, doable opportunities. The big picture
encompasses vision, mission, goals and positioning, and the
process deals with them in a natural evolutionary way. Then
you move to the second, more defined level, identifying the
most lucrative target groups with whom you must position
your company and brand relative to your competition.
Finally, you distill further, identifying and converting specific
opportunities into projects that are actionable and measurable.
This moves you from blue sky (or moon view) to down-to-
earth pragmatic action (daily view).

Obviously, much of innovation centers on opportunity –
uncovering it, seizing it, and converting it.

From Webster's dictionary:

Opportun' ity *noun*: **a favorable juncture of circumstances, a favorable occasion, a good chance.**

An opportunity is what you identify it to be, and this will differ by the needs of your customers, the type of products or services your company offers, and the effectiveness of your processes. Of course, it will also depend on the change that your organization is committed to bringing about.

Opportunities exist on many levels, and while we can't define your opportunities for you, this process helps you understand the levels that you must be able to think through in order to arrive at the opportunities that best suit your organization. It is an integrated process that involves continually exploring and developing new opportunities through a cycle of innovating, leveraging and implementing.

Chapter 11

Step One
Engaging Emotions, Not Numbers

Foresight grows from insight and it starts with reflection.

Ken Tencer

There are many studies and books that, in my loose interpretation, tell us that individual decisions are based to a large extent, consciously or subconsciously, on the collectivity of our life's experience. So based on this principle, we start our process by exploring the past.

Foresight is everything. That's why we begin with reflection

Looking back helps you understand the forces behind the growth you've achieved. It helps you identify the factors that led to the start of the business, the launching of products and the adding of services. This important first step gets you beyond today's day-to-day mindset and allows you to rediscover the rational and emotional building blocks of the business, and the entrepreneurial passion and innovation that fueled it. Inspiration always has a starting point, and where you will be tomorrow can draw heavily on those original sparks.

If you want to succeed you should strike out on new paths, rather than travel the worn paths of accepted success.

Anita Roddick, founder, The Body Shop

Every business success — whether rooted in how the company got started or in some of its later triumphs — begins as an idea in someone's mind. It is honed through vision and the courage needed to make things happen. And success emerges through a mix of foresight, intuition, insight, innovation, head-splitting thinking and the sheer will to act. When you revisit how you got to where you are today, you will nearly always find the cornerstones, insights and ingenuity that made the difference.

Many years ago I had the opportunity to speak with Jennifer Mulholland, founder and President of a manufacturer and importer of outdoor casual furniture. She recounted for me the unusual tale of how her company was inspired — and how it got started.

In 1991, Jennifer was between jobs and decided to travel to the Far East to visit a long-time friend. During that trip, Jennifer was struck by the richness and expression of the traditional local cultures. In particular, she was taken by the beauty of their creations, the textures, and the melding of woods and metals that were explored and crafted into their furnishings.

To pass the time on the long flight back, Jennifer leafed through a variety of home and decor magazines. As she perused the offerings she noticed how boring North American backyard furniture was, and how limited the range of products. Everything seemed aimed either at the low end, created from cheap, disposable materials, or at the very high-

On a personal note, Jennifer's story reinforced for me why my first degree was in marketing and my second in finance. If you can't identify a customer and market need, then numbers are irrelevant.

end: utilitarian products offering "lifetime" guarantee. There seemed to be no middle ground and certainly nothing to spark the consumer's imagination.

Having a strong background in marketing and design, Jennifer knew then and there what she would do next in her career: Create a design-inspired line of outdoor furniture based on rich, exotic woods that enhanced and transformed the backyard into a true extension and expression of the home – all at an accessible price-point.

"I have found that inspiration comes at different times and in many ways," says Jennifer. "Unfortunately, we are not always open to it when it does appear, and then the opportunity is lost."

As we go through our model, you will note that the catalyst in Jennifer's history was the emotional stage. It hinged on the intuitive recognition of connecting specific benefits to the customer's emotional needs for beauty, comfort and value. Understanding that personal component is critical because too often, business professionals think only from a linear, chronological or dollars-and-sense perspective, and miss the emotional links. Jennifer saw the *emotional* void in the outdoor furniture market.

On a personal note, Jennifer's story reinforced for me why my first degree was in marketing and my second in finance. If you can't identify a customer and market need, then numbers are irrelevant.

To this point, I have always remembered a key concept I learned in an undergrad course I took called Consumer Behaviour. That concept is *cognitive dissonance*, which loosely defined and applied, is about the gap between a consumer's behaviour and their feelings. Someone may be behaving in a certain way (using a product) but they may not be happy

Cognitive dissonance, which loosely defined and applied, is about the gap between a consumer's behaviour and their feelings. Someone may be behaving in a certain way (using a product) but they may not be happy about it. They may, secretly or openly, want a better solution to their problem, but they don't know where or how to find it. It is in this gap where innovation thrives – identifying and addressing consumers' longings that are not yet reflected in their behaviour.

about it. They may, secretly or openly, want a better solution to their problem, but they don't know where or how to find it. It is in this gap where innovation thrives – identifying and addressing consumers' longings that are not yet reflected in their behaviour. Gillette is one company that has mastered filling these gaps. When we used the old single-blade razor it was "good enough" – better than its predecessor, and all we had. A few nicks here and there were accepted. Until the two-blade razor came along. And then three blades. Gillette addressed a behavioural problem that consumers were tolerating, even though they didn't like it, because there didn't seem to be any other solution. This also happens with new models of automobiles. Who knew we needed a rear-view camera on our car until we had it? How about the problem of opening the back hatch door of your SUV while your arms are full of groceries? After numerous struggles and a few dropped bags, some automakers finally introduced the auto-latch opener, which you tap with your toe and "open sesame."

So as we move through this first stage of innovation, we are rediscovering the solutions that we have provided to customers in the past, and beginning to uncover problems for which we can provide new solutions going forward.

History in three parts

The first goal of Step One is to develop a collective understanding of your company's history and evolution. As part of this process, we look at your history from three points of view: chronology, emotion and revenue. This then forms the basis for "blue-sky" thinking.

Part I: Chronological history

Your chronological history provides a foundational timeline that allows everyone to see clearly the growth and development of the firm. It gives you a record of important dates; changes and introductions of products and services; points of innovation; critical turning points; and major shifts in the company's direction. From this you can create a collective perception of how the company became what it is today. Inherent in this is an examination of its strengths and weaknesses, and an opportunity to explore ways of generating new growth.

Part II: Emotional history

Emotions are an underlying driver of a company and its culture. It's essential that everyone understand the genesis of the company's inspiration and emotional drive, and the 'turning-point' decisions that it has made. From this, everyone can become more emotionally engaged in the company's goals and vision, which in turn, fuels the individual entrepreneurial spirit and innovative thinking.

Also, this process allows you to find out how employees perceive the company, why they joined and why they are here. To maximize leverage, it is not enough to just have the viewpoint of the founder or CEO, or even a handful of leaders; it must come from everyone. Employees, especially those who have been there for many years, are an invaluable part of a firm's "memory" and can provide emotional insights on its history and growth. This is part of mapping a way forward.

Part III: Revenue history

Revenue history reveals future potential and pitfalls. Understanding the source of revenues and profits across your history allows you to look forward and assess whether these sources are likely to grow or diminish in future. You can see trends, patterns and anomalies that tell the story about what you did and didn't do, and how and where the company generated revenues and profits. You also explore factors behind these trends, such as technology, laws and regulations, product life cycles, competitor's actions, changing consumer markets and innovation.

A historic revenue picture provides a platform on which everyone can combine past and future thinking through "the numbers". Too often we either get stuck in the present need or leap too quickly to future projections without first realizing that it all ties together in a continuum of opportunity.

Background for blue-skying

These visits to your past help everyone understand your organization's strengths and passions – the capabilities that account for your 90% -- the foundation for your next innovation breakthroughs. Understanding this historical perspective helps you envision a different future and identify the stepping-stones needed to get there. This gives you the requisite foundation for Step 2, "blue-skying," making it relevant and contextual versus haphazard. This shared insight is the common denominator on which everyone can "blue-sky" the future. Past and future are always linked: while reviewing your history, discuss and make notes on future considerations as you go along. Pose questions such as:

- Where do you see the future of the business?
- What new things might customers need?
- What new customers might we need?
- How do you see us getting there?
- What would we need to resource that?

History is revealing if you are prepared to open up your minds to the future.

Vision is the art of seeing what is invisible to others.

Jonathan Swift (1667-1745)

Hypothetical objectives

Most companies have established specific objectives – financial, marketing, sales – which at this stage we call "hypothetical objectives." The reason is simple. This process puts all your objectives, strategies and tactics through a rigorous series of "tests" that are based on customer-centric benefits, market-centric strategies and existing assets; therefore, until they are "tested" they are considered hypothetical.

These hypothetical objectives give you a baseline to work from. They can be as ambitious as you like, but it is important to make them pragmatic. Don't talk about expanding into 20 new countries in the next three years or doubling the business every six months unless you believe that there is a good chance you can achieve it. In turn, don't set easy objectives that can lead to "average" performance and complacency. Both are ultimately demotivating, counterproductive and damaging.

As you proceed, use three timeframes in your blue-sky thinking: 1 year; 3 to 5 years; 10 years. Your objectives can stem from many facets of the business and will include, but not be limited to, such things as:

- Corporate revenue
- Revenue by division or product
- Revenue growth rate
- Market share

- New market penetration
- Customer base
- Geographic growth

With history in hand and a range of hypothetical new objectives, it's time to broaden the exploration.

Chapter

12

➡

Step Two
Exploring what you can be,
not what you are

*It's about pursuing beliefs
and transforming passions.*

John Paulo Cardoso

The crucible for entrepreneurial and innovative thinking is the exploratory mind and its incessant questioning: "What if?" "Why not?" As the view turns from the past to looking at the potential, entrepreneurs constantly ask, "What can be?"

Entrepreneurs and innovators are ahead of the curve, ahead of the market, ahead of current thinking. By contrast, good managers tend to be just slightly ahead of current thinking, average managers demonstrate current thinking, and managers who are behind the curve simply fall behind.

You've got to think about the big things while you're doing the small things, so that all the small things go in the right direction.

*Alvin Toffler,
American writer and futurist*

Entrepreneurs and innovators are ahead of the curve, ahead of the market, ahead of current thinking. By contrast, good managers tend to be just slightly ahead of current thinking, average managers demonstrate current thinking, and managers who are behind the curve simply fall behind.

For example, the traditional approach to rebranding is based on trying to understand "what the company is," and then coming up with a corporate identity and pithy slogan to communicate that current state. Our methodology generates far more insight and depth, and is also more pragmatic. It explores *what you can be* versus simply *what you are*. For instance, taking your company from sales of $50 million to $100 million usually requires more than adding a blue chair to your product line and a new slogan to your brochure.

I have discovered, over and over, that success is rooted in what you believe your business can be and do, not simply in what you are offering today. This exploration stage is about pursuing those beliefs and transforming the passion that got you here into renewed, bigger benefits for your customers, and opportunities for you.

Benefit-driven thinking

The outcome from this stage of the process is the platform on which corporate vision, strategic intent and blue-sky ideas coalesce. Customer-centric thinking (versus product/service-centric) means the future is not about what you physically do or make, but addressing what the customer needs and wants to achieve, in their business or personal lives. Most companies have an inherent product-centric bias that is difficult to shed. That is why exploring and understanding the customer-centric perspective opens up a new horizon of *what could be*.

What business are you really in?

Big question. Many companies have difficulty answering it correctly. The exploring and prioritizing of benefits allows you to define or redefine the business you are in.

Some of these benefits are obvious, while others are less apparent and yet just as important. Still others have been lost in the push and pull of growth and the day-to-day operational scramble. By applying the *Corporate Features and Benefits Model* (see page 158), you can look at the benefits that your products and services provide to your customers. We have added a couple of steps to this model – personification and impact – to really help you to bring your business' benefits 'to life'.

In this model, a company's "features" refers to the full offering of the products and services that it provides to its customer. The continuum that we are building is on the next page.

Now, let's explore the corporate features and benefits.

1) What are the main *corporate features* of the products and services that you are selling to your customers (e.g., accounting services, books, cars, hedge trimming, software)? List them all.

2) What are the main *tangible benefits* of your company, products and services? Define them as specifically as possible (e.g., drive faster, last longer, taste better, higher resale value, pay over-time, etc.).

3) What are the key *emotional benefits* that customers derive from your company, products and services? Essentially, what ego satisfaction do they achieve by using your products or services? Define these benefits (e.g., reflects their lifestyle; trend setters; belong to an "in-group;" perceived to be more intelligent, better educated, in-the-know; feel good about how they look; etc.).

4) Once you've explored all the features and benefits of your products from a customer perspective, then you *personify* them. We use personification because it provides character and personality to this long list of inanimate features and benefits. Ultimately, business is about relationships, and every business needs an identifiable character and personality. To identify your

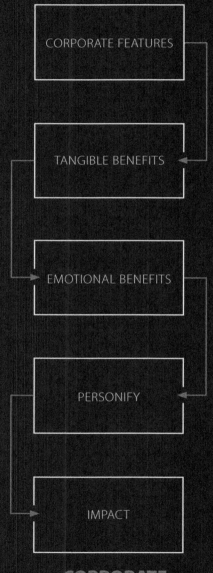

CORPORATE FEATURES

TANGIBLE BENEFITS

EMOTIONAL BENEFITS

PERSONIFY

IMPACT

CORPORATE
features and benefits model.

business' personality (traits), simply ask the participants in the exercise to name well-known things or people that they feel have similar characteristics to your company (i.e., strength, elegance, beauty, function, cost, etc.). For example: Cars (Mercedes or Chevrolet?); Animals (Lion or Cheetah); People (George Clooney or James Gandolfini); fashion (Versace or GAP) movies; songs; etc.

5) Review your findings from these exploratory steps and distill them into an *impact statement* that summarizes your business' full customer influence.

Examples of how benefits + personification become impact statements:

- Revlon is not about making cosmetics;
  it's about **selling hope**

- Wellpoint is not about providing medical services;
  it's about **helping people to live better longer**.

- *Today's Parent* magazine is not about family reading;
  it's about helping parents **live with less guilt**.

- Disney is not about movies and theme parks;
  it's about **fun, family entertainment**.

- Starbucks is not about coffee;
  it's about **coming together to meet in-person**.

Defining vision and mission

Now, with your customer-centric benefits, personality traits and impact statement in hand, you can align your vision and mission.

It is critical to understand the difference between a vision and mission statement. All too often, I find they are not properly understood or written. Remember, these are statements (not autobiographies). You want them to be clear, concise and memorable.

Below are excerpts from what I consider one of the clearest explanations, which came from a presentation by strategy consultant Bill Birnbaum to the American Management Association, published online at www.birnbaumassociates.com.

> **Vision Statement:** "... a vision is not true in the present, but only in the future. Your strategy team will need to develop a compelling vision of the future. A vision that your employees will enthusiastically embrace —because the vision is worthy and because it challenges them to grow."

> **Mission Statement:** "Your mission describes what business you're in and who your customer is. As such, it captures the very essence of your enterprise – its relationship with its customer ... Mission has both an internal and an external dimension ... it also lists the functions the company performs ... also includes the necessary external dimension. It identifies the customer ... and it cites the company's 'market position' – the reason why customers would prefer to buy products and services from the company."

Sticking to – versus getting back to – your core business

Once you have articulated your business' impact, vision and mission, you are beginning to clearly understand and better define your core business. It's an essential cornerstone on which to drive growth and a better practice than shown by many companies who tend to zig and zag, get off course, and then have to work themselves back to their core.

With this inherent understanding of your business, you are also moving closer to a list of actionable, measurable and relevant opportunities.

A few who understand

Always remember that this whole thing was started with a dream and a mouse.

Walt Disney

Disney

Disney wouldn't be Disney if Walt had thought that the company's product was just five-minute cartoons rather than seeing the company as being in the business of fun family entertainment (short for movies, TV, merchandise and theme parks). Walt may not have imagined the extent of the retailing and merchandising empire that would evolve but he realized that the real "pixie dust" was about staying true to your core. He knew success would stem from being consistent at every level of the business and building a brand based on consumer delight. The Disney company still lives by that magic, and continues to deliver more and more customer benefits by creating innovation around 90% of its core capabilities (cartoons led to features which led to owning mythologies, which led to TV which led to Disneyland – and so on). Even some of the company's more startling recent moves, from building its own town in Celebration, Fl.,[7] to buying the Star Wars properties from George Lucas are direct manifestations of that original vision, mission and brand.

[7] *Disney's town Celebration website: http://www.celebration.fl.us/*

Apple

Apple wouldn't be a global behemoth if Steve Jobs and Steve Wozniak had not first thought about redefining the concept of the personal computer. What if they had accepted the assumption of the times that computers were massive, expensive machines unsuited for individual use? But they didn't stop there. Where would Apple be today if it had just thought of itself as a manufacturer of personal desktop computers rather than creating design-enhanced personal technologies? And where would Apple be if it were not customer-centric rather than internally business and profit-centric (the vision of former CEO John Sculley)? Apple didn't just redefine its business. It redefined an industry. And continues to do so (i.e., music, retailing).

Lululemon Athletica

Lululemon hasn't thrived by manufacturing pieces of clothing but through building a culture of well-being. Its mission states the company's primary intent: *Creating components for people to live a longer, healthier, more fun life.* Notice, no mention of athletic clothing itself. And take a look at their core values listed below – they see themselves as much more than a vendor of clothing.

lululemon core values[8]

Quality: Our customers want to buy our product again.

Product: We create components designed by athletes for athletes.

Integrity: We do what we say we will do when we say we will do it. If we cannot keep our promise, we immediately contact all parties and set new by-when dates.

---

[8] *lululemon website: www. lululemon.com*

Balance: There is no separation between health, family and work. You love every minute of your life.

Entrepreneurship: We treat and pay employees as though they run their own business.

Greatness: We create the possibility of greatness in people because it makes us great. Mediocrity undermines greatness.

Fun: When I die, I want to die like my grandmother who died peacefully in her sleep. Not screaming like all the passengers in her car.

Home Hardware

Home Hardware, a Canada-wide retailer, has exemplified the success that accrues from having recognized a growing market and building by adding an innovative twist that better serves your market. Years ago they recognized the growth in the do-it-yourself (DIY) market and tapped into this trend by providing information and guidance to help customers do things themselves. They also partnered that platform with a community-based store location strategy providing friendly, neighborhood advice and product solutions for your home. This has helped them to become a leader in the Canadian DIY market – instead of continuing to be just another supplier of commodity hardware products, competing on price and location.

Nutrition House

Nutrition House has pioneered the natural health and wellness industry. For the past 23 years the company has built its credentials through scientific research, quality ingredients and expert in-store counseling. Nutrition House provides the health information, products and services you need to make sound nutritional decisions about your life. To be a pioneer like Nutrition House, you must position your company beyond just selling products. It's not about inventory, it's about being with your customers where they live, every day. The company positions itself as understanding and "proposing" a different way of living and eating. This alternative approach involves living life in a proactive way and applying natural solutions rather than the traditional "hope-you-feel-better" panacea of modern medicine. Strategically, this has helped Nutrition House leverage its knowledge and expertise into larger-format stores, international distribution of its products and extended product offerings, including healthier food choices and ready-to-enjoy natural snacks and drinks. All this is a natural expansion and leverage of Nutrition House's inherent core competencies. As they say, "Better Health Lives Here."

Our mission is to 'Lead and Foster Well-Being Responsibly.' As such, education plays a large role in our organization. We feel it's important to not just sell products, but to provide natural health solutions. These include lifestyle changes, proper nutrition through diet and supplementation, exercise, and rest.

Wayne Parent, President, Nutrition House

Industrial companies have impact, too

A manufacturer perceived itself as being in the business of making and distributing bottles and caps for consumer and industrial products – until it moved to rethinking the benefits it provides to its end-users. First, it realized it wasn't selling plastic components; it was selling its customers new possibilities. Possibilities that make those customers' jobs easier. The company became a co-visionary with its customers, enhancing their growth potential as well as its own. Now its communications material speaks in the language of its customers and focuses on the benefits it brings to the table. At the same time, its communications imagery moved away from a product-centric view of empty bottles and caps to showing the consumer products that their bottles and caps became when decorated and put on shelves.

It's not about size

As you can see from these examples, you don't have to be a multinational company (i.e., Disney or Apple) to understand and apply the principles in this book. In fact, it is often easier if you are a smaller, more flexible, entrepreneurial-minded group. In larger companies, innovation is often more effectively done by starting within a business unit, division or large department.

Remember, this exploratory step is about kick-starting a customer-centric mindset and, I repeat, one of our guiding principles is: *If you are not going to cause a disturbance and change customers' lives, stay in bed*.

Everybody can explore

Customer-centric thinking is never limited. Every product or service can make a difference in the lives of customers. Just ask the people who brought you California Raisins, Sunkist oranges or Chiquita bananas. People didn't simply buy them to eat fruit; they chose them because they had been branded as natural and fun. Remember how the raisin industry repositioned raisins as "Nature's candy?" Don't tell me that didn't impact millions of parents who were trying to convince their kids to eat fruit instead of candy.

Every product or service can make a difference in the lives of customers. Just ask the people who brought you California Raisins, Sunkist oranges or Chiquita bananas.

Once you can get your people to move beyond traditional product-centric thinking, you have a chance to build brand equity by establishing a customer-centric hypothesis and beginning to create a more relevant brand – testing it against your customers and the competition, and then honing a positioning statement that resonates in your customers' souls.

Not every company is going to put a man on the moon. But the ones that understand themselves and their market are the ones that change peoples' lives. They are the ones that grow. Did Apple change its customers' lives? Did Disney? Revlon? Home Hardware? Nutrition House? You bet they did – and they continue to do so. Are you next?

Chapter 13

Chapter

•

Step Three
Building a relevant brand

Creating and sustaining a relevant brand is critical to sustainable growth. Without it, your brand will always be an afterthought in customers' minds— if it's thought of at all.

John Paulo Cardoso

The trail of clown-faced shopping bags

As a young boy and a newcomer to Canada, living in Toronto south of Mirvish Village, I (John Paulo) remember following a trail of shoppers down Markham Street with their clown-faced shopping bags to see where the heck they were coming from. They led me to the ultimate Toronto shopping experience, Honest Ed's, which is one of the largest (for its time) and most unusual discount department stores you will ever see. Honest Ed's had a huge neon sign encompassing an entire city block, and made up of 23,000 light bulbs. It also employed catchy slogans such as, "Come in and get lost!" and "At Honest Ed's, only the floors are crooked!" Ed's featured value-priced products and merchandise in a kitschy and nostalgic circus theme. The inside of the store, with its vintage bargain-basement feel, still reminds us of a time before the big-box stores came to town. Ed's gained fame for its marketing stunts, including loss-leader specials, free turkey giveaways and extravagant yearly street parties on the birthday of founder Ed Mirvish.

After more than 60 years, Honest Ed's is more than a store; it's an established and successful brand. Its brand architecture brings together vision, voice and benefits that together provide the inspiration and personality of a lasting brand. (So why isn't there an Honest Ed's in every town? Mirvish turned down offers to expand or franchise his store, choosing hands-on retail management over corporate success.) Honest to its customers and its core self, Honest Ed's remains memorable, instantly recognizable and a cultural icon that has innate emotional appeal and community relevance.

Successful brands are unique and beyond compare. They are always innovative, instantly recognizable and built on an emotional connection with their customers. They are distinct, exude personality, and resonate deeply with a loyal following. Simply put, brand is the personification of your products and services, enabling customers to engage and build a relationship with it.

Are your customers still following a trail back to you decades later?

Building a relevant brand

When it comes to creating and sustaining a successful brand, it's easier to fail than succeed. The market dumpsters are full of brands that started out with a chance to win but lost their way and became irrelevant.

What is a relevant brand? It's always relevant to its customers. It delivers what clients want in a way that is compelling and clearly differentiated from the competition.

As I mentioned earlier, branding is about the relationships you build with your customers. And innovation – the continuous improvement or introduction of new products and services – is what keeps the brand and your company's relationship with its customers fresh.

And that is why the chapter on branding forms such a big part of a book on innovation. As I mentioned earlier, branding is about the relationships you build with your customers. And innovation – the continuous improvement or introduction of new products and services – is what keeps the brand and your company's relationship with its customers fresh. Whether you are building a company or selling products or services, they should all be deliberately and strategically branded to ensure they find a relevant and lucrative market and a lasting place in the mind of your customers.

Many business leaders over-think innovation. They believe that devising better products and services is a daunting, expensive and scientific process. In reality, it can be as simple as watching your customers use your products and figuring out how to make the user-experience easier, richer and more beneficial.

Case in point: personal-finance software giant Intuit Inc. of Mountain View, Calif. Since its founding in 1983, the $4-billion-a-year maker of QuickBooks and TurboTax has built its growth almost entirely on grassroots innovation.

Intuit founder Scott Cook, a former marketing manager with Procter & Gamble, wasn't the first to develop personal finance software. But he was probably the first to phone hundreds of consumers in both Palo Alto, Ca., and Winnetka, Ill. (chosen as two sample affluent communities) to ask what they liked and disliked about managing their personal finances. The ensuing product, Quicken, prospered because it was simpler and easier to use than its competitors. In light of Silicon Valley's lust for "first-mover advantage," Cook called his customer-intelligence tactics "47th-mover advantage."

More significantly, Cook also started the practice he calls "following customers home." He and other Intuit staff would ask to sit in consumers' kitchen and dens and watch them pay their bills. "We wanted our software to be intuitive," he says. "We wanted to have an unfair advantage over competitors and that unfair advantage was usability." With every product release, Intuit still sends engineers out to interview customers using their product. And indeed, most staff members still take a turn tracking the customer experience. Intuit CEO Brad Smith says the company does 10,000 hours of "Follow Me Home" research a year. "I do 60 hours myself," he adds. "We want to find out what gets in the customer's way. That's our strategy."

When Smith became CEO in 2008, he realized his toughest task would be to make sure that Cook's instinct for first-hand customer research remained a driving force at Intuit, even after Cook moved upstairs to chair the executive committee. "Scott Cook is a visionary like Bill Gates or Steve Jobs," says Smith. "But it is all in his head. He turned customer-driven innovation into an organizational capability." So Smith has developed a multi-layered process to ensure that client-driven innovation remains the company's lifeblood. It's one that many companies can learn from.

Intuit gives participating staff 10% "unstructured time" to work in teams on independent innovation projects. Experience has taught that these "Design for Delight" teams should have just four to six people – or as Smith says, "No more than two pizzas can feed." Team members include a range of skills, such as engineers, designers and marketers. "They go broad to go narrow," says Smith.

Smith says these innovation teams are expected to develop at least seven different ideas – to make sure they don't just fall in love with one idea. Then they explore three more deeply before selecting the single best idea to develop. Teams usually get six weeks to turn bare ideas into working concepts; as Smith says, "Innovation is born of constraint." For best results, Intuit teams start consumer testing long before their products are finished. Smith says Intuit has learned that the more complete a prototype looks and feels, the more reluctant customers will be to critique it. "If it's still wrapped in duct tape, they will help you fix it."

To cover expenses, Smith controls a "CEO Innovation Fund" that may hand out $20,000 or more to support new product development. "We'll fund it for 90 days to see if it's then worth investing in." The money is carefully doled out to ensure that both short-term and long-term innovations are nurtured. Innovations in existing products, the mainstream of the business, get 60% of total R&D funding; "adolescent" growth sectors, such as online services and mobile apps, get 30% and 10% of funding must go to over-the-horizon ideas. Indeed, all executives are expected to keep an eye on the future: executive compensation is tied in part to revenue from products less than three years old.

Smith says Intuit's institutionalized innovation has helped the company grow revenues by double-digits even in a slumping economy. And the new-product pipeline, he said in 2012, "is now five times bigger than it was last year."

Finally, Intuit makes a point of celebrating not just successful innovations, but well intended failures as well. "You have to celebrate failure as much as you celebrate success," says Smith. "Your best learning comes from things that don't work." By shining a light on things that don't work, he says, "we make sure you won't make the same mistake twice. We want you to make a bunch of new mistakes." Every year, Intuit hands out the Scott Cook Innovation Awards, for the most successful innovations of the year and, adds Smith, "for the experiments we learned the most from."

A brand is not your logo

Most people think a brand is just a name and logo. As you know by now, it's not. A brand is an instinctive, subconscious, gut response based on how someone feels about a product or service. It is much more than the things that make up a brand identity (logos, colors, fonts, images or characters), which are important symbols used to reflect and ignite the good feelings someone has for a product or company. A brand is the representation and culmination of everything an organization believes in, what it stands for and the direction it is heading. *It must have real value and meaning for its customers and everyone else.* What would the world's biggest product, Coca-Cola, be without its brand identity? Brown fizzy sugar water. Coca-Cola sells its experience and not just its features. How did Apple become the No. 1 brand in the world? Yes, its logo and image are exquisite, but its "Think Different" brand goes deep into its customers' psyches.

Why should you care? In Marty Neumeier's book, *The Brand Gap*, he quotes an Interbrand study that reminds us in concrete terms that your business is worth more with a strong brand.[9] Today, the value of a brand shows up on companies' balance sheets. Coke's market cap without a brand is estimated at $50 billion and with its brand it's $120 billion. And what about the Microsoft brand? Often considered stodgy compared to Apple, the giant of PCs is redoing its brand image. Perhaps it might have something to do with the fact that its market capitalization is only about 40% ($250 billion) of Apple's ($600 billion). And Microsoft is doing this not on its traditional strength in engineering but through design. Design is being suffused through numerous products, including the new Windows 8 operating system and its new tablet, Surface – the first PC device Microsoft has manufactured in its nearly 40-year history.[10]

[9] *Marty Neumeier, The Brand Gap, Peachpit a division of Pearson Education, p.12*
[10] *"Microsoft Wipes the Slate Clean," Fast Company, Oct. 2012, p. 122-124*

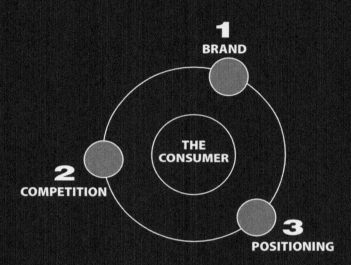

1
BRAND

THE
CONSUMER

2
COMPETITION

3
POSITIONING

BUILDING
a relevant brand.

Regardless of a company's size, brand has a huge impact. Damage to a brand can undermine value, which will show up on the P&L in lost sales or the balance sheet when it comes time to sell. Probably no one knows the extent of the "brand hit" (pun intended) to the National Football League brand following the NFL's use of replacement officials early in the 2012 season. But there's no doubt that brand was damaged, simply due to a lack of care shown about the value of the product on the field, and a lack of foresight by the league's owners in letting a minor labor dispute affect the game. They obviously do not understand the value inherent in a great brand – although the NFL likely will suffer less than "normal" companies because it operates with limited competition.

Consistency and predictability of the "brand experience" is crucial. Every contact and touch a customer experiences means something. Think of it this way. Everyone in your organization is doing one of two things every day: Strengthening or weakening your brand.

Brands are created for three basic reasons:

1. Differentiate from other brands
2. Simplify and strengthen the purchasing decision
3. Build a trusted relationship with customers

In short: Brand = Relationship = Stronger Business

The 90% Rule model not only helps you build your brand, it ensures that you continue to reinforce its relevance in the marketplace.

Getting it right and keeping it relevant

First, we want to focus on the components of a brand and bring structure to building a sustainable brand. Doing this will help you know how to:

- Define your brand.

- Determine what makes it relevant to your most financially significant customer groups.

- Develop the most effective ways to communicate those benefits so that they are perceived to be different from other products and services in your category.

- Ensure that your brand remains relevant.

You can get fame quickly. But building a brand with real depth is no quick fix.

Carl Lyons, Marketing Director, www.lastminute.com

Too many companies think they understand their brand when they really don't. When we apply our model, many clients are surprised at how "off" their understanding of their own brand is. Too many assumptions; too little vigilance.

There are many factors that encumber a brand's chance for success. Some are so obvious that I have trouble understanding why companies allow them to happen.

- Not clearly defining the brand and aligning it with the company's strengths, thereby never being able to deliver the "brand promise." Example: Many companies try to brand themselves as low-cost providers but they can't consistently compete with the big guys (i.e., Wal-Mart, Costco) who can be, and are, the low-cost leaders.

- Not tracking consumer trends, needs and wants, and adapting and refining the brand accordingly.

- Not taking the time to understand customers' specific wants and needs so as to ensure that the brand is continually accepted.

- Not taking the time to do a comprehensive competitive survey to understand the different ways in which customers can satisfy their needs through competitors' products and services (unless of course you *plan* to be a "me too" provider).

It's not about you: It's customer-centric, not egocentric

I don't think I can ever say this enough: "It's not about you." I am always amazed at how disconnected a company can get from this fundamental premise. You don't buy what you make; you make the products to sell to other people, so it's their vote that counts. Whatever you produce, it is for someone else, so your brand better be relevant to that someone.

> *There is only one boss; the customer.*
> *And he can fire everybody in the company from the chairman on down, simply by spending his money somewhere else.*
>
> Sam Walton, founder, Wal-Mart

It's too easy to put you and the company and your products or services at the center of your thinking because it's "where you live." It is what you do and know best. But you and all your "stuff" are not all-important. Stop ignoring the elephant in the room (smack-dab in the middle of your planning and operations), the customer. The customer, not you, stands at the center of the *90% Rule* model – because customer needs should drive every decision you make. Understanding what your customers want requires constant vigilance. After all, their needs and wants change constantly and if your brand is to be relevant it must adapt. You need to track the customer, continually.

Whatever the customer wants

I was once on a conference call to help stage the relaunch of a national store brand for a leading retail chain. Because many of the client's products often required explanation to

Customers can't always imagine what doesn't exist but they can always articulate their 'pain-points" quite clearly.

the shopper, a member of the chain's merchandising team asked if they should set up the specific section to suit the needs of the store owners or the in-store shopping patterns of the customer. One of the storeowners piped in to say, "Set up the section to the liking of the customer, and I'll adapt." He had it right. This is an example of day-to-day "right thinking." Think like the customer. Think like the customer. Think like the customer.

Pause and think: Do you constantly think like the customer, and act accordingly?

The idea is to befriend your customers and get to know not only what they want, but what they might need in the future. Quite often, the important things that you learn are subtle, which is why you need a systematic means of capturing new information and ideas. Henry Ford once said, "If I had asked my customers what they wanted, they would have asked for a faster horse." I think that if he had asked, his customers would have actually said a faster, safer and warmer way to travel. Customers can't always imagine what doesn't exist but they can always articulate their 'pain-points" quite clearly. I often hear people downplay research by saying, "How can you research something that customers have never seen or don't know about (e.g., a car)? How can they have a valid answer?"

As market-research expert Marion Plunkett of Plunkett Communications Inc. explains, research can help you identify problems that customers are having with products or services currently in the marketplace. (Remember Gillette and its understanding of the problems of shaving.) While customers might occasionally offer suggestions, it's really up to you to design solutions that work for them and for your organization. Customers can tell you where they are now and where they've been, but not where to go in the future. That's your job. That's the job of innovative thinking.

Remember back in Chapter 11 where we noted that cognitive dissonance (the gap between behavior and emotion) is where innovation lives and thrives? Listening to the "voice of the customer"(VOC) is a big part of that, and it can help identify many needs. Here are a few examples of needs-driven solutions to think about:

- A mode of travel to get to the destination faster, safer, dryer and warmer than their old nag Gus. Result? The first Ford.

- A way for vacationers to avoid pulling out their wallets or signing for drinks every five minutes when they're on vacation. Result? The carefree all-inclusive approach to vacations at any level of sophistication you choose: three, four or five stars.

- An easier way of packing school lunches – recognizing that most school-lunch sandwiches are of consistent shape and size – and easier to use than traditional pull and tear plastic wrap. Result? Sandwich bags.

- A fun, convenient and less fattening way to serve and enjoy cake: cake pops.

The point is that research is a way of listening to and observing customers as they identify needs (met or unmet) that can be translated into new products and services. Customers always speak in terms of benefits they are looking for, seldom about product features or services.

Research should never be used the way a drunkard uses a lamp post—more for support than illumination.

David Ogilvy, British marketing executive

The most common, dismissive reason for not doing research is, "80% of what research tells us we already know." Ignore that. It may be true, but it misses the point. It's often the next 10% that you weren't sure of that gets confirmed and provides illumination, especially when you do solid information-seeking research. Most importantly, it's the final 10% that you did not know that is really worthwhile because it can yield critical insights into what your customers need or might need in the future – the cognitive gap and a cornerstone of innovation. The market never lies; it will always tell you what to create if you listen closely.

Brands have always been about the relationship between product and user ... A brand signals a set of expectations and a core understanding that drives everything.

Shelly Lazarus,
Chairperson, Ogilvy & Mather Worldwide (2000)

Building a brand begins and ends in your customer's mind

I want to talk a little bit about a number of crucial factors in creating and sustaining a brand.

Relevance lost

Lots of companies develop brands but many can't sustain them. If a brand fails it is because it has either never been relevant to the customer or it has lost its relevance along the way – usually because the market and the customer changed and the brand did not. If your brand isn't relevant to what the customer cares about, then the customer isn't going to care about your irrelevant brand. And if you want to be relevant, you had best start with knowing your customer and your market.

The first step we've covered. You identified your brand's tangible benefits, emotional benefits, personification and brand impact by running the exercises in the previous chapter. I don't like to ask people straight out to define their brand because it's a big question and not easy to answer "off the top." However, together with the brand impact discussion and development of a brand statement, you are able to define a customer-centric brand and business. That's the first step (we'll get back to that exercise in a moment).

As I walk through the steps of brand development, please remember that the goal of this book is not to provide a dissertation on branding. Rather, it's to provide three things:

i) A jolt of reality: How leverage and The 90% Rule can play a critical role in the evolutionary growth of your business (of which branding is an integral part).

ii) A jolt of thinking: Entrepreneurial thinking is the kind of thinking that drives innovation, pursues opportunities and leverages current assets (which depend on a strong brand).

iii) A jolt of pragmatism: A process for rethinking, reunderstanding and reaccelerating growth – the elusive next 10% (for which a strong brand is critical).

The focus and work on benefits helps you get away from product-centric thinking. Whether your shoes come in blue or black is secondary to the emotional and functional benefits and experience that you provide to the customer who wears your shoes. The old adage, "If the shoe fits, wear it," might be more accurately stated in marketing terms as, "If the shoe fits your emotional needs, buy it." In other words, understand how the benefits obtained from wearing your shoes will help change your customer's life. Yet I am amazed at how many companies I meet whose entire organization operates around

The old adage, "If the shoe fits, wear it," might be more accurately stated in marketing terms as, "If the shoe fits your emotional needs, buy it." In other words, understand how the benefits obtained from wearing your shoes will help change your customer's life.

product-centric thinking – producing certain colors of shoes because blue sold well last year or black is more efficient to produce. And assuming no one would ever want magenta.

Remember, the predominant force in the customer's buying process is based on emotions, not pragmatism. Feelings greatly influence buying decisions and often override logic. Branding is about building a relationship around your customer's feelings. A brand is experienced by the customer as a set of characteristics and values that they associate with your products or services. Some of those characteristics go to the physical nature of your products (i.e., quality, price) and your name, logo or wordmark, while others go to the values that a customer holds and expects to be reinforced by your products or services, or from working with your company. The essence of a brand is determined more by visceral and intuitive responses than pragmatic motivations.

Brand Architecture®

Great buildings, the ones that leave a lasting impression while serving a functional purpose, begin with a solid blueprint, based on information assembled by the engineering and architectural team. In the marketing world, we often hear the term "Brand Architecture" (a registered trademark of Plunkett Communications Inc.), and it's an accurate term when properly understood. The dictionary defines an architect as somebody whose job it is to design buildings. That's a little bland for my liking – sort of like calling the Beatles "a band." I would say that brilliant architecture transforms the landscape in unique and creative ways, ways that touch us emotionally and intellectually. So too does effective brand architecture coalesce around vision, knowledge, experience, emotions, needs and benefits. It creates a voice and feel that collectively provides inspiration, personality and the structure that determines a lasting brand. Every successful brand is built on solid and well-defined brand architecture.

Every breath you take

Brand Architecture is designed on the premise that every touch point of a brand is interconnected. A brand is a living, breathing entity. I often say that every brand architect should have as a theme song the platinum hit by the Police, *Every Breath You Take*[11] (" ... every breath you take, every move you make, I'll be watching you"). Because its every move is under scrutiny in the marketplace, it must offer authenticity in representation and consistency in delivery—especially in this age of social media, where every critic has a megaphone. That means never underestimating the importance of every touch point in brand creation, delivery and communications. How your brand looks and performs ("every breath it takes") should be part of your daily thinking.

Making friends

Like a person, your brand has a personality and make-up that it takes into the marketplace and develops over time. Analogous to people, brands are born and grow and can become quite individualistic. Like people, they also adopt and reflect belief systems (of their company) that identify how they are going to perform in certain situations. As people, we decide what we're going to wear to outwardly express who we are and we choose to eat, drink and behave in a certain manner. Together, our decisions make us individuals whom others perceive in a certain way, and either befriend or not. Think back to your first day of school and how both first impressions and lasting characteristics mattered as you made friends and built relationships. How a brand makes friends is akin to that. The objective is to develop your brand in such a way that it will

[11] *Every Breath You Take from 1983 album Synchronicity by The Police*

make the most friends. If you get it right (and refine it along the way), you will probably have many successful long-term relationships. With seven billion people in the world, you can't befriend everyone, and ditto for the millions of brands looking for relationships with all those people. But, if you identify and pay attention to your customers, you can become their "best friend."

To stretch the friend analogy, it's obvious that popularity counts (backed by good character and values) in gaining friends and building relationships. But do not underestimate how easy it is to lose favor. Customers truly know the value of a friendship and if your brand is not relevant to their needs then they have little allegiance – and other choices. This is critical in both business-to-business and business-to-consumer marketing. The customer is bombarded with choices – there are always options – and in the end they will want to know, and be associated with, the brands (friends) they value the most and believe are most relevant to their life.

Making the ordinary extraordinary: Sketchley Cleaners

Early in my career I had the opportunity to work for one of the pioneers of Canadian advertising, Jerry Goodis. At the time, his work was recognized internationally as exceptionally creative, and founded on the principles of branding. I believe that much of his work ("At Speedy you're a somebody") stands today as relevant, insightful and, in many cases, audacious.

One of the more challenging accounts at the agency was the Canadian chain of Sketchley Cleaners. This was at a time in the late-1980s when we were realizing more and more the extent by which "equity value" could be built into a brand. Sure, we had already witnessed decades of products, in all categories, that had grown their brands (e.g., Coca-Cola, McDonalds, IBM, Oreos) and Goodis had created his share of memorable brands: Wonderbra, Hush Puppies, Canadian Club, Speedy Muffler, Harvey's. But this wave was different. We were seeing commodities such as raisins from California become singing and dancing sensations, and cookies in bright yellow bags with "No Name" become as well known as the longstanding brand-names. And then came the "No Frills" and "President's Choice" brands (now expanded as far as financial services). Branding was being extended to an almost endless array of products and services. And in the midst of this proliferation, the Goodis Agency was faced with branding what was almost universally perceived as a commodity, dry cleaning.

The vision was to create the first uniquely branded chain of dry cleaners in Canada. One that instilled trust and confidence in the consumer – something usually lacking between consumers and a chain of dry cleaners. There were a few individual dry cleaners positioned to offer high quality, but chains were perceived as offering a commodity service.

After extensive examination and defining of what was important to its customers, Sketchley identified a key gap: inconsistent and often poor quality delivered by the cleaner and low expectation in the mind of the consumer. There was a perception that "you got what you paid for." Customers stated that their clothes were important to them, but they had low expectations when it came to how the cleaners treated their clothes. This led to the strategy of Sketchley offering three levels of service, each offering a different combination of quality and price. The customer could choose the price/ value they wanted. In turn, this was tied to a positioning and brand statement that emphasized the fact that Sketchley cared about its customers' clothes (it was not a commodity), and that cleaning quality really mattered. Sketchley used its graphic identity symbol of Three Penguins and created three levels of quality (good, better, best) with the positioning line: We know you love your clothes. It was the quintessential recognition of the customers' feelings about their appearance and the clothes that articulated their personal identities. Sketchley's pitch went beyond the customers' clothes to their personal appearance and lifestyle. I wrote the brand strategy, which in essence said: If a dry-cleaning chain could express its recognition of this emotional attachment and imbed it in its brand, then it could differentiate itself from the competition and build a unique customer-centric relationship – and a strong Sketchley brand.

What can your brand be?

Once you have identified the key *tangible* and *emotional* benefits inherent in your products or services and established what business you are in, you have the foundation on which to build a your brand.

To confirm that your brand is relevant, we look at three key components

    I. Customer

    II. Competition

    III. Positioning

I. Customer: Honing in on your most lucrative target groups

You begin by generating a comprehensive list of current and potential target customers and then identify the ones that you think have the highest and best potential.

Development steps:

1) A useful place to start your market analysis to understand current and potential customer groups is with what we call, "life of engagement." This enables

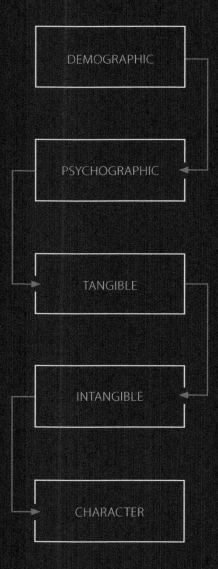

you to understand how your customer engages with your company, products or services over the long term. Understanding this behavior makes it easier to hone in on key target markets and segmentation criteria (i.e., demographic, psychographic, geographic).

Life engagement examples:

- A toothpaste company understood that to engage customers for life, it needed to reach them from the first time they brushed their teeth. It was first to market with junior toothpaste and children's brushes, and first to offer incremental products (whiteners, floss) at all stages of oral health.

  Life engagement:

  Toddler ➡ Junior ➡ Teenager ➡ Young Adult ➡ Adult ➡ Senior

- An association engaged in professional development and certification begins reaching people while they are in high school through their introduction to careers in business and industry. It continues to provide a range of information, from continuing education for all to specific services aimed at the executive suite.

  Life engagement:

  High school ➡ College ➡ Entry ➡ Mid-Mgmt. ➡ Sr. Mgmt ➡ Exec. Suite

2) Delineate your target markets using demographic, psychographic and geographic attributes. To be clear, adults 18-49 who live in Washington, DC is not a sufficient delineation. You must look at and create personifications of your various target groups based on what they like and don't like – all the emotional and

practical appeals. What they think, watch, eat, wear, visit, experience, and so on. Essentially, we are profiling your customer, just as we did your company.

3) Once you have identified segmentation criteria and target groups, you need to compare what your current and potential customers want in relation to the tangible, intangible and esoteric characteristics that your brand offers. This lets you discuss what it is you are capable of offering to each target and, more importantly, the wants and needs that you are *not* currently capable of meeting.

NOTE: If you do not have strong customer information, then use this exercise to create a hypothesis about what they want and then confirm your assumptions through further qualitative and quantitative research.

Before moving on, I want to reemphasize point 2). You must go deeper than simply describing where your customers live or how old they are. Customer profiles describe the target group in detail. Think of it this way. If your company is personified as Santa Claus then it probably shouldn't go after customer groups that see themselves as Scrooge. Or a Chevrolet pursue Cadillac customers.

II. Competition: Who else is speaking?

"Oh, we have no real competition" is one of the most dangerous proclamations I hear when it comes to marketing. (And I've heard it said so many times). I remember one time a group of clothing executives described their new brand as unique and pretty much competitor-free. I looked around the room and commented that although their line had not yet been launched, no one in the room was naked. They got the point.

There is *always* competition. And if, on a rare occasion, you have no *direct* competition — at that particular moment (i.e., the NFL oligopoly, or Xerox in the copying business in the 1960s) — you can rest assured you will meet it soon enough. Many a company has fallen victim to the folly of this "non-competition syndrome." In fact, the NFL could lose marginally interested or newly introduced fans. The smaller the business, the more vulnerable you are to this dangerous assumption.

We ignore the competition at our peril.

- Xerox had a brand name so prominent that it became a verb used in every office. When people wanted a copy they would say, "Xerox this for me." But Xerox became complacent, and when the competition struck, it took decades to recover.

- With its unassailable brand name, Aspirin thought it didn't have competition either. You know them, the leading pain-relief medication that became an afterthought to Advil and Tylenol. Aspirin only rebounded when it was found to be helpful in prevention of heart attacks.

Competition is a given. Believe it.

I don't want this to sound like a knock on the people who said they had no competition, because I'm sure they believed it. And in some cases they were probably thinking only about direct competitors, although I dispute that notion, too. I liken this thinking to the legal concept of conflict of interest. I once asked my lawyer what constituted conflict of interest and he said, "Anything that the other party thinks it is." This may not be the fully articulated legal definition but the point is clear:

conflict and competition are in the mind of the beholder. And when it comes to marketing, this non-competition perception will bring the beholder a lot of unwanted conflict. I live by a different assumption: Competition is a given.

The pertinent questions should be: What types of competition exist? At what level? Direct or indirect? Now and in the future? (The latter is very important.) Then, of course, you have to think through which of these competitors are most applicable to you. When assessing competition, the first level of questions is straightforward:

- Who do you come across in your daily work life?
- Who are you selling against?
- Who exhibits at the same trade shows as you?
- Who books into your customers' visitors' logs before or after you?
- Who has websites that address similar customer needs?
- Who is advertising what and where?
- Who do your customers mention? (Ask them.)

Watching the competition

As in the case of Xerox and Aspirin, there is hope for once-leading brands that are assailed by new competitors or market forces.

"Precise as a Swiss watch" is a world-renowned cliché but by the 1980s, the Swiss watch industry was no longer ticking smoothly. Centuries-old craftsmanship was losing ground to cheap Japanese electronics in a market that valued price over tradition. But as industries around the world collapsed in the face of Asian competition, the Swiss watchmakers resolved to save their sector.

Step one was to face facts. To rescue the watch industry, so essential to Switzerland's international reputation, old-time craftsmanship was no longer enough. In the face of foreign competition, Swiss watchmakers would have to become more efficient, competitive, and market-savvy.

The revolution began with consultant Nicolas Hayek, who engineered the 1983 merger of two troubled giants, ASUAG (which included the Longines and Rado brands) and SSIH (makers of Omega and Tissot) into one company known as SMH. Hayek demanded that the new company retool to develop cheaper modular components and invest in more stylish design to combat the low labor costs of overseas producers.

The result was the Swatch, which originally meant "Second Watch," and is now understood to mean "Swiss watch," showing how successfully the brand has been resurrected. With fun and cheeky styles, garish plastic components and a $30-$50 price tag, the Swatch gave consumers an affordable alternative to Seiko and other Japanese manufacturers. Inside, the quartz watch had been reinvented with new materials and assembly technology, reducing the number of components from 91 to 51—and slashing production costs by 80%.

By 1986, SMH was recognized as the world's leading watchmaker and Hayek had taken control of the company as chairman and CEO. By emphasizing new technology, production innovation and design, and employing marketing alliances with leading international designers, Swatch's analog watches have held their own in a digital world.

Today, the Swatch brand includes children's models, ultra-thin and Scuba watches, metal and plastic watches, seasonally-themed products and even Swatch jewelry. Recognizing the power of the brand it had created, SMH renamed itself

Swatch Group in 1998. Yet it still markets most of the world's most high-end watch brands, including Breguet, Blancpain, Glashütte Original, Omega, Certina, Mido and Calvin Klein.

Today, Swatch's manufacturing innovations show up in everything from telecommunications to microelectronics – and even in the modular assembly of Daimler AG's Smart Car, a project actually launched by Swatch. The company's success against all odds proves that when a company pools its expertise with the latest technology and a passion for marketing, new opportunities and innovation are not just possible, they're abundant.

Hang out with the competition

If you haven't recently done it, now is the time to find out everything you can about your competition. It's easy to get started, right in your own office. The power of observation can produce informational gems. The best way to take a closer look at your competition is to bring them into your office and let them hang out for a while. Put them up on your wall, literally. Pin up their ads, brochures, web pages, mission statements, product samples, price lists, locations and any other intelligence you can find. Then stare at them for a while. You will be amazed at what you can learn if you make an objective assessment of what you see.

Competitive overview process

Your assessment of the competition can start simply by evaluating (on a scale of 1 to 10) what you and your team think of their overall company, their main points and their products/services. Be honest. Leave your ego at the door.

- What is their image, their voice or their brand – or lack thereof?

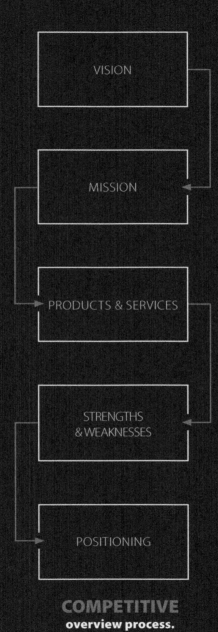

- Do they identify their vision and mission? Does it make an impression?
- Who are they speaking to, customers?
- How do they talk about their products and services?
- How is their overall presentation, look and message?
- Do they have a brand? Is it strong, weak, consistent or non-existent?
- Are their key messages strong, average, weak or even valid?
- What do they say about their competition (you), directly or implied?
- How do their main points compare to yours?
- How do you perceive them to be positioned?
- How well do they tell their story and make their case?
- Where do you think they are missing the boat?
- Most importantly, what can you say or do that is both relevant and different from the customers' perspective?

At the end of this process, formalize your findings. Create a *Competition Overview* that compiles and compares the information about what you know about the competitors and your company.

After your in-office analysis, and as part of building your brand architecture, you can do a more in-depth analysis of the competition (i.e., customer interviews, focus groups, quantitative research, etc.).

How do you stack up?

Never get tired of asking the question: "What is it that I am offering that is different from my competition, and will change my customers' lives?"

Not to pick on one specific industry sector, but manufacturers are usually the worst offenders when it comes to promoting what they think is important (*features*) versus the most relevant customer *benefits*. In their brochures, they love to feature beauty shot after beauty shot of their products. They often lead with close-ups and specifications. They seem to ignore the fact that what they are manufacturing usually looks frighteningly like what their competitors make. Then there's the obligatory plant tour shots. Let's be real for a minute. If you produce millions of widgets a year and sell them to a host of Fortune 500 companies and you are also ISO certified, it is safe to say that people who are contacting you assume that you have a plant somewhere; one that is probably pretty big and reasonably well run. So unless you are the only one in your industry with a plant that makes products, you can probably keep its picture off the front of your brochure – and off the back page, too. None of this does anything to make your brand relevant.

Where is your point of differentiation? What can you do or say to set your products apart? Because people are busy today, and every day, so you'd better be making a first impression that connects rather than just looking like another ripple in the ocean. Otherwise, you might just as well stay in bed because not only is your brand irrelevant, it doesn't exist in the mind of your customers.

I understand that it is important for manufacturers to provide technical specifications and to show that they are equal to the competition, but this repetition *ad nauseam* is not relevant. These seemingly minor mistakes can kill a brand before it is born. And not understanding all the little things that aggregate into creating a memorable brand can prevent you from ever making a lasting impression in customers' minds. It can damage your position in the market and lead to the demise of your brand, even your business.

Little things make a difference

First, let's remember the old saying, "Little things can make a big difference." We all have examples from our own experience of the little things that make us loyal to certain stores, products and services. Or make us never go back. One such example for me is my cellular provider. I am sure you remember how phone companies locked you into long-term contracts and rates that would remain high with no relief unless you paid a penalty to get out of the contract, usually by switching providers. Where is the benefit to the business in that? Make a little more in the short term but lose the customer after only a year or two. It's no wonder that providers were constantly churning customers. But my service provider has managed to keep me for many years now. Why? Because I get calls on a regular basis from its customer care department. They say that they have been monitoring the use of my business' phones over the last few months and have found a less expensive monthly package for me and if I agree to it today, they will discount the overages from the previous month. That is an excellent customer-centric benefit, and in return I am a loyal customer. Another customer-centric business is any restaurant that deletes a charge from my bill with no questions asked when I have had any sort of problem with the food or service. The result? I'll come back – in part to return the respect they showed me.

The 90% Rule is based on leverage, and the requisite cornerstone for maximizing leverage is the strength of your brand. That strength has a great deal to do with how you position it against the competition.

III. Positioning: If it isn't relevant and memorable, it's lost

In their landmark book, *Positioning: The Battle for Your Mind*, Al Ries and Jack Trout explained positioning this way: "To succeed in our over-communicated society, a company must create a position in the prospect's mind. A position that takes into consideration not only a company's strengths and weaknesses, but those of its competitors as well".[12] The focus on customer thinking needs to be converted into your brand positioning by pursuing the main question: *What can your brand be that is most relevant to the customer and clearly differentiates it from what is already available in the market?* Sketchley did exactly this.

Always look for options that you believe your organization has the capability of building, delivering, servicing and embodying. These options form a hypothesis and provide a test platform for determining which brand concept can win the most friends and influence the most people. Here are a few obvious examples of questions that help define your brand options:

- Most exclusive brand or a brand for the masses?
- Safest car or most stylish?
- Freshest and fastest to market or biggest selection?
- Full service or self-serve?
- Carefree and light, or serious?
- Top-of-the-line and as-good-as-the-best for a little less?
- Long-lasting or less durable and less costly?
- Brand leader or generic substitute?

This part of the process helps you figure out and bring together the two sides of the equation: What the consumer will want, perceive, experience, believe and always gravitate toward; and what you can deliver on, profitably.

[12] *Positioning: The Battle for Your Mind, Al Ries and Jack Trout, page 29*

Positioning and branding are inextricable. A positioning statement links both what the customer needs and the benefits you offer; your brand must create that positioning in the mind of the customers. Positioning evolves from the process of exploring, rethinking and redefining; it rises like cream to the surface as you stir and remix the collective thinking about your business and brand.

Nothing expresses a brand better than a successful positioning exercise translated into a memorable positioning slogan. We all remember our favorites, and the good ones transcend time:

"We try harder" (Avis)

"A Kodak moment" (Kodak)

"It's the real thing" (Coca Cola)

"At Speedy you're a somebody"
(Speedy Auto Services)

"We know you love your clothes"
(Sketchley Cleaners)

"We care about the shape you're in" (Wonderbra)

"Just slightly ahead of our time" (Panasonic)

"I Love New York" (New York City and State)

"The Ultimate Driving Experience" (BMW)

"Technology you can enjoy" (Honda)

"I am Canadian" (Molson Canadian)

"I'm lovin' it" (McDonalds)

"Have it your way" (Burger King)

"Harvey's makes a hamburger a beautiful thing"
(Harvey's)

"Real women have real curves" (Dove)

"Because you're worth it" (L'Oreal)

"Because owners care" (Westjet Airlines)

"Buy Canadian, the rest of the world does" (Canadian Club)

"The man in the Hathaway shirt" (Hathaway Shirts)

"Think small" (Volkswagen)

You don't have to be an international brand to have an effective positioning and slogan. One of the more memorable slogans that I've heard is for a plumbing contractor: "Number one in the number two business."

Going back over what a few of my favorite marketing authors and speakers have said, I have paraphrased the essence of why positioning is so important.

> *If you offer the same thing as your competitor for the same amount of money backed by the same level of service, chances are you are pretty much the same as everybody else and you're not going to be winning much new business. It may seem obvious, but let's face it: not every company in a sector can have the best people, best engineering, best service, best product, best price and offer the best same thing. Reality is, every product or service has to carve out a recognizable position for itself in the mind of the consumers, and then fight like hell to attain it, maintain it, strengthen it.*

Determine positioning, then make a statement

Do not confuse positioning points with a positioning slogan. Both are essential, but the "points" are singular ideas that communicate where you want to be in the customer's mind. They precede the slogan. The slogan drives home your positioning in creative and memorable ways.

Brand ➡ *positioning point(s)* ➡ *positioning slogan*

Here are examples of slogans created from, and built on, strong positioning that we are all familiar with:

- Lever 2000 soap ➡ cleansing, deodorizing and moisturizing ➡

  For all your body parts

- Southwest Airlines ➡ less for much less ➡

  We give people the freedom to fly

- BMW ➡ the best ➡ performance ➡

  The ultimate driving experience

- Coke ➡ *always first* ➡ *number one*

  The real thing

Most of our clients have worked through this process, and the results are always a better, more compelling positioning. Here is an example of how we worked through the process in our own company. I share it with you because it helped us understand how difficult, but necessary, it is to take a step back and reexamine our own company. Yes, we practice what we preach, regularly.

At Spyder Works we went through the process of asking ourselves: What can we do to position ourselves differently? And, of course, we found that the bulk of the answer came from our customers.

Over the past 20 years, we have come to embrace a business development platform focused on "branding + innovation," and assumed the mantle of "boutique with influence."

What branding + innovation means to our customers is best articulated in the words of a senior executive, "Spyder Works provides us a venue to look at ourselves more strategically, to take a step back and imagine us differently in the marketplace."

In our words, Spyder Works' mission is to provide the skills, tools and confidence to corporate leaders to enable them to reimagine and grow their businesses and brands in the marketplace.

This is in keeping with our vision, which is to reimagine anything (businesses, brands, products, services or processes). This has struck a chord with executives who face the day-to-day and long-term challenges of remaining relevant and fresh in today's turbulent marketplace. It is relevant and powerful in all facets of their business development – sales, marketing, innovation, finance, leverage and growth.

As we explored our accumulation of years building different businesses and working with clients to help them build businesses, we found what one client called our "sweet spot." We dug a little deeper.

We hung a lot of our competitors up on the office wall and realized that most of those in our space came at it either with big company positioning (usually experience-based at the top and under-experienced below) or as a single-source solution (specialized consulting in research or strategic planning or design or advertising).

We learned from our customers (ranging from individuals building their own businesses to executives responsible for divisions of large companies) that what they wanted and needed most was a "partner" with a handful of critical attributes:

- A hands-on group who bring to the table relevant, senior business thinking that is immediately applicable.
- A group that can help them see what their business and brand can be – and can help make it happen.
- A group that has the capacity to provide both the up-front planning and thinking as well as the ongoing

implementation services (strategy, branding and across-the-board communications).

- A flexible group that adapts to specific needs – both immediate ("fire fighting") and longer-term (sustainable growth).
- A fully engaged extension of the management team.
- A group that provides senior expertise and insight into pressing go/no-go decision points in the organization's business development.
- A group that although a temporary part of the team, makes sure that the new, collective thinking sticks long after they have left (i.e., install a systematic process).
- A group that is affordable on a cost/value basis and helps us get the most out of what we are already good at.
- A group that delivers on time and on budget.

Our customers needed a range of in-depth, experienced thinking that directly related to specific decision-making and ongoing action. They needed "plug-in partners" who could bring to them new, objective and innovative *thinking and doing*.

We recognized our customers' exasperation with the gap between strategic thinking and execution. In an ideal world, such gaps would not exist. In reality, however, clients were used to hiring two or three different firms to help solve a wide range of problems related to their lack of expertise in areas such as research, strategy, design and communications. Consequently, there was no seamless connection between thinking and doing, which produced inconsistent strategies, weak branding and sub-par communications.

As a result, Spyder Works positioned itself as a partner that brings to its clients a step-by-step process to refine their growth plans and develop innovative strategies, relevant branding and integrated design that consistently embodies the company across all internal and external communications. This thinking is the cornerstone of the *90% Rule*, which in itself is a strategic process that leads to tactical implementation. It is a fundamental part of our trademarked model, *Building Business by Design*®.

Not only does the positioning differentiate us in the marketplace, but most importantly, it provides our clients with a built-in, sustainable process that ties the market directly to their vision, goals, strategies, brand and communications. This confident, consistent and integrated approach creates new leverage for ongoing, sustainable growth.

I once received a salient compliment from a long-time client who had worked with many consultants and agencies. She said, "I like working with you guys, because there's no fluff."

IV. Pricing strategy

As we have seen, there are many different ways to differentiate your company and its products or services from the competition. However, most people seem to start in the same place: price. I don't recommend this strategy. It's a common mistake that needs to be addressed by almost every company.

Why? Primarily because it reinforces our thinking as product-centric. Most companies focus on cost and set product prices simply based on their own costs and margins, rather than understanding the inherent value of their products from the customer's perspective. By not taking a customer-centric view in the first place, we ignore the value *that's perceived by the customer* - which is often higher than the marked-up value of a commodity.

Price and pricing are a balancing act between cost (what it costs to produce and deliver) and value (what customers perceive and are willing to pay). How much is too much? How much is not enough? Your pricing is the proverbial moving target that you must strategically determine and then continually monitor and manage. Price should be set according to both *the value of a product and your to-market costs. Getting the highest price for your products* should be part of your overall growth strategy, as identified by assessing your best opportunities.

If your best opportunities are in the higher end of the market then quality and pricing become a critical part of strategy, and part of the value you want your brand to reflect. It is not a tactical add-on. Price by itself – as in "cheaper" – is not enough; there must be clear benefits layered into what you offer. As we all know, strong branding can achieve premium pricing (Heinz, Sony, Mont Blanc, Ray-Ban, Whirlpool, Apple, Canada Goose), and premium pricing can complement and strengthen branding.

The adage, "You get what you pay for" may be old but, it certainly isn't tired. I have never wanted to be the lowest-price supplier at anything that I do, even when I manufactured commodities. And I certainly avoid that tactic when I'm proposing to help other people build value. There can only be one lowest-cost supplier in a market, and all other competitors are positioned somewhere else -- or they die trying to be what they can't be. As mentioned, Wal-Mart and Costco are the leaders in mass-market discount retail. Everyone else needs a different pricing strategy and one that works in close concert with their positioning (e.g., Target, Walgreens, Sears, The Bay).

When you have a clear positioning you need to connect a clear, complementary pricing strategy to it, because positioning and price are inextricably linked.

Final check

Scour your history, especially the emotional history, and look for "gems" those strengths, capabilities or consistent wins that point the way to a more successful future. Then look at these gems through the customers' eyes. Talk to customers and prospects. They will anchor your positioning statement. What satisfied customers say about you, in their own words, can help define your positioning in a new, more customer-centric way. And springboard you to a more relevant and powerful brand.

Chapter

14

Step Four
Identifying and Ranking
Opportunities

**Leverage is a powerful tool. Use it well
and use it often.**

Ken Tencer

Entrepreneurial thinking assumes that there is never a shortage of opportunities just a perceived shortage of resources. If you do your due diligence to identify your best opportunities, as well as the potential of the resources you already have, you will uncover the leverage you need to succeed.

If you take only one thing away from this book, I hope it is the notion that your business can benefit from a growth strategy built on *leveraging current assets and logical next-step opportunities* rather than the relentless acquisition of new assets and pursuit of ever-changing strategies and tactics based on short-term performance. That's simply chasing fragmented growth and reckless hope.

If you take only one thing away from this book, I hope it is the notion that your business can benefit from a growth strategy built on leveraging current assets and logical next-step opportunities rather than the relentless acquisition of new assets and pursuit of ever-changing strategies and tactics based on short-term performance.

The application of the *90% Rule* gives you two fundamental benefits:

1) It creates a clear and essential context in which you can make strategic decisions (Steps One, Two, Three).

2) It allows you to identify your best opportunities and leverage your current assets against them.

He who pursues many things accomplishes nothing.

Anonymous

Defining opportunity

There is no dearth of opportunities in business; they are everywhere. The key is in defining the few that are most applicable to you and your business. Here is our definition of a business opportunity.

Business opportunity: A set of circumstances that makes it possible to accomplish business goals that are actionable and measurable.

To seize your best opportunities, you need to evaluate and organize potential opportunities into highest-and-best-return groups.

This step is designed to help you identify and isolate the optimum range of opportunities. Each business is different; we have had clients start with more than 50 "blue-sky" opportunities and then build a plan around as few as two. Others have ended up with as many as 18.

The essence of strategic reasoning is the ability to creatively challenge "the tyranny of the given" (Kao, 1996) and to generate new and unique ways of understanding and doing things.

De Wit and Meyer, authors, Strategy Synthesis

Converging opportunities

We call this part of the process "grounded blue-skying" because you move from blue-sky ideas down to the optimum number of opportunities. When reviewing your history, vision and mission, you will have identified lots of opportunities that seem worth pursuing. But now you will end up with specific, measurable opportunities that you can pursue with added confidence because you know who you are targeting, what you believe they want, and what your organization is at least 90% capable of delivering.

Let's get to work.

Highest-and-best-return

In this step, you create an *Opportunity Assessment* by brainstorming all the opportunities that fit with your vision and mission, and match your core markets. The brainstorming is guided by three broad factors (see below: global, market, financial) and four key marketing questions, which are founded on the same analytical principles of Ansoff's matrix[13] and other similar tools and models.

Four leveraging questions

All your blue-sky opportunities need the following four overarching questions applied to them during the process of convergence.

#1: Market Penetration

What can you do to *increase sales to existing customers* in existing markets with existing products?

Determine new uses for the same product. Examples:

- Use of baking soda in a refrigerator
- Serving eggs for dinner

[13] Ansoff, Igor (1957), "Strategies for Diversification", Harvard Business Review, 35(5), September-October, 113-124. Examples were also adapted from Papadopoulos, Nicolas, William Zikmund, and Michael D'Amico (1988), Marketing (Toronto, ON: John Wiley & Sons Canada), Ch. 9.

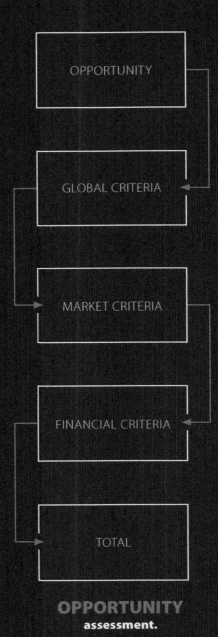

OPPORTUNITY
assessment.

- New stores in current markets – improve accessibility
- Smaller half bottles of wine (at more than ½ the price)
- McCafé: elevating coffee from menu item to signature category
- Best Buy 'on the go' airport-based vending machines
- Every frequent flyer/loyalty program ever launched

#2: Market Development

What can you do to develop *new sales in existing markets by attracting new customers?*

Match current products and services to "fence sitters" and new prospects. Consider any adjacent or incremental opportunities that emerge from your analysis. Examples:

- Running shoes marketed as walking shoes to seniors
- PCs to the high-school market
- Tim Hortons goes beyond doughnuts and adds sandwiches
- Tide introduces clothes-washing pouches for ease of use

#3: Product Development

What can you do to *increase sales to existing customers in existing markets with new products?*

Develop and offer modified or new products to current markets. Examples:

- Salads at fast-food restaurants
- Seminars and "lunch and learns," instead of full-length courses

- Professional sports teams selling branded clothing
- Introduction of organic home cleaners

#4: Product Diversification

What can you do to *increase sales to new customers in new markets with new products*?

Master product diversification by marketing new products to current and new customers. Examples:

- Introduction of G Adventures
  (for adventurous travelers)
- Starbucks' purchase of music company
  Hear Music to play and sell CDs in stores
- Apple Computer introduces the iMac, iPod,
  iPhone, iPad
- Dyson transitions air flow technology to industrial
  hand dryers and 'fans'

Prioritizing

- Generate an extensive list of opportunities that you can consider based on who you are targeting and what the customer wants.
- Provide each of the participants five 'stars' to place beside the five opportunities that they believe most relevant.
- Next list the Top 10 opportunities as identified by star allocation.

After you identify and rank opportunities according to the five-star allocation, then further rank each opportunity according to three criteria: global (company's high-level, strategic direction), market (sales and marketing targets and ratios) and financial (top-line revenue, contribution, productivity ratios and net profit). The sub-criteria below (bullet-points) are only a few ideas to get you started, there are many others that your team may think of or already have in place.

The one thing that is extremely important is that you rank each opportunity against all three categories. Don't fall into the trap of saying, "great idea, not in-keeping with the long-term vision of the company but I am positive that I will make so much profit from this idea, so quickly, that I just have to go for it and then I'll worry about getting back on-strategy next quarter". Remember, the story about company's selling off non-core assets? Well, I am convinced that it starts by cutting corners or, in this case, cutting out ranking categories to get the answer that you want.

1) Global factors:
- In keeping with your vision
- In keeping with your mission
- In keeping with positioning
- Your "gut check" (intuition)

2) Market factors:
- Length of the selling cycle
- Potential for long-term growth
- Customer and market group
- Potential competition
- Expertise
- Time to market

3) Financial factors:
- Impact on revenue
- Impact on cash flow
- Margin contribution
- Required investment (low requirement is worth 10)
- Required personnel (low requirement is 10)

Once you have matched the opportunities to your strategies, you can transform strategy into tactical action. Then you're ready to put together a go-to-market plan of action.

Top 10

By the end of the *Opportunity Assessment* you want to arrive at your own "Top 10" best opportunities (give or take a couple). And then there is one more step: The top three (give or take). These are always custom-tailored to your particular needs and situation. Whether you have two or 10, each opportunity must be anchored in the twin principles of the 90% Rule – *it is your highest and best potential for growth, and It can be highly leveraged using your current assets.*

A cautionary trail

The path between strategic and tactical thinking is filled with bumps and excuses, particularly the established, encrusted, assumptive and subjective ones that rationalize why old opportunities are better than new ones. We know it takes a tough objective assessment – the key word being *objective* – to boil many opportunities down to just a handful of the best. Too often, companies have convoluted reasons for hanging on to some customers and chasing old opportunities – for all the wrong reasons. For example:

- "He, she or it has been a customer for a hundred years"
- "X product generates high sales volumes"
  (left unspoken is its low margin)
- "Bob Is a favorite customer" (usually based on personal relationship, not a business case)
- "We can't afford to lose the cash flow"
- "They're a subsidiary of our biggest customer."

Unless the ranking of opportunities is done thoroughly and objectively, and matched to your strategy and current capabilities, you will have little chance of converting even the best of strategies into effective, highly leveraged, tactical execution.

Chapter

15

■

Step Five
Building the Plan

Innovation by its very definition is about introducing the new and navigating the unknown. It begs a thoughtful plan of action.

Ken Tencer

Entrepreneurs do not walk in lockstep with conventional wisdom or follow traditional maps; they chart their own course (ask anyone, from Christopher Columbus to Sir Richard Branson). If you intend to have a say in shaping your future, it's important to understand how to shape what you offer so that it best fits the map of the marketplace.

The great discoveries are usually obvious.

Philip B. Crosby, author of Quality is Free

The opportunity process: Turning opportunity into success

The greater the opportunity, the more that you need to plan for success. Too often I find that we get so excited about our new ideas that we believe that they will magically walk themselves to market. But, it does not work that way. Innovation by its very definition is about bringing something new to the market.

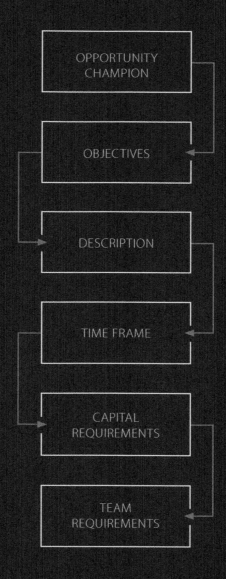

THE OPPORTUNITY
process.

The one thing that many people forget to ask during the strategic process is: What are we going to need to get this done?

This translates to more unknowns. Bringing an opportunity to market requires a leader, a team and a well crafted plan that outlines timelines, capital requirements and checkpoints.

Mapping opportunity

The *Opportunity Matrix* is a simple tool that enables you to assess the opportunity-identification work you have done to date. It also drives consensus-building and cross-disciplinary team "buy-in" by including a full complement of people in the process of assessing, contributing and allocating internal resources to the new opportunities.

Opportunities don't come to fruition because of the work of a few people. Executing on the best opportunities requires knowledge, thinking and passion from all functions of your company. What teams will your opportunities require? HR? Engineering? R&D? Marketing? Sales? Manufacturing? Finance? All of the above? These discussions identify the strength of available resources and how best to allocate them. For example, if the majority of opportunities are short-term and depend on human capital, it raises the question of whether you have the people in place to achieve your objectives. Conversely, if many of the opportunities are in the long-term, it means looking at longer-term financial options.

The one thing that many people forget to ask during the strategic process is: What are we going to need to get this done?

Opportunity Matrix

Your go-to-market resource requirements and considerations are linked to the quadrants on the matrix. Within the Opportunity Matrix are:

- **Quadrant 1:** Short-term implementation based on financial capital

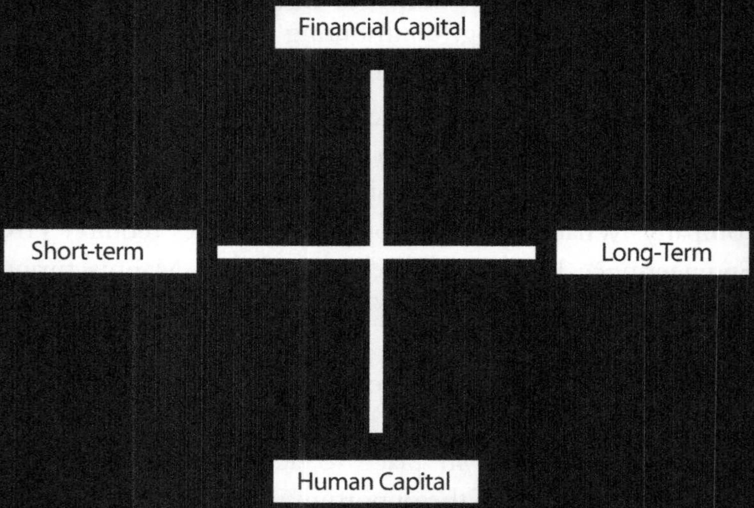

OPPORTUNITY
matrix.

- **Quadrant 2:** Long-term implementation based on financial capital
- **Quadrant 3:** Long-term implementation based on human capital
- **Quadrant 4:** Short-term implementation based on human capital

If all the opportunities you have identified rank in the top-right quadrant, then developing all these opportunities will take a lot of money and time. Conversely, if everything is in the top-left quadrant, then you need a lot of money plus everything needs to be done tomorrow. Similar challenges can be derived for the quadrants that relate to the need for human capital.

> *You can't design and build a building in bits and pieces. But you can design and build a city, one building at a time. t's time to be resourceful.*
>
> *John Paulo Cardoso*

The goal of the whole exercise is to come up with a manageable flow of opportunities. So if you find that too many of your new opportunities are clustering, it's time to drill down deeper and see how you can reconfigure the opportunities and/or break them into stages.

In the following list of successful growth strategies, note how often the word "outsourcing" comes up. Contracting out vital services you need to move ahead may cost a little more in the short term, but it will be far less expensive and risky than doing it all yourself. Frankly, you may never be able to do it all yourself. There is a reason that companies outsource key functions such as payroll and HR exist; it enables them to focus on their core competencies. In fact, some companies, such as Nike, outsource all of their manufacturing, so that they can focus on their core strengths (design and marketing) every day.

- A bath and body-care company outsources high-season filling and packaging.
- A landscaping company explores interior, lobby gardens through outsourcing.
- An institute contracts an outside trainer to kick-start its custom-training division.
- A bottle manufacturer begins a major growth drive by outsourcing the industrial-design portion of the process.
- A furniture company outsources delivery and installation as demand spikes, until the firm is sure that the new level of demand is sustainable.

My eleventh-grade geometry teacher and rugby coach would always remind us (loudly), "There are many ways to skin a cat." Excusing the inappropriate metaphor, he was right. Your job is to harness the power of your interdisciplinary team and find the ways, paths and steps to achieve what you want with what you have. This is not a time for guesswork or all-or-nothing decision-making. You want to chart your course sensibly but boldly. That takes deliberation and collaboration by everyone involved.

Marc Ecko: Edge and authenticity

Marc Ecko had a clear map of what he saw in the marketplace. Just as Lacoste has its crocodile and Ralph Lauren has his polo pony, Eckō Unltd. has a rhinoceros as its symbol. To young urban Americans looking for "street cred," the incongruous rhino offers proof positive that they're wearing original Eckō hoodies, jeans, t-shirts or sneakers—the hottest name in casual wear.

Ecko started out in business by selling custom spray-painted t-shirts while still a high-school student in Lakewood, New Jersey. By 1993 his colorful graffiti-inspired designs started catching the attention of prominent hip-hop artists, and Ecko abandoned Rutgers University to sell street clothes full-time. When a line of rhino-themed t-shirts sold out fast, Ecko knew he had found his key visual element. A rhinoceros, you say, doesn't exactly scream "urban America"? That's the idea. "I think good design makes you scratch your head," says Ecko. "It's the nonlinear bit, the bit that's not logical."

Within three years Marc Eckō Enterprises had $16 million in sales, but sky-high debt. An angel investor helped the company work down its debt—but his most important contribution was to recognize that Eckō wasn't a t-shirt company, but a lifestyle brand. Switching his focus from creating cool shirt designs to devising radical marketing schemes, Ecko turned his company from a money-loser into a lifestyle machine. Eschewing industry fashion shows, for instance, he doubled sales by creating commando teams to sell Eckō clothes right on the street. And he broadened his appeal by expanding into jeans, hoodies, and women's and children's fashions with an urban edge.

Today Eckō is an international super-brand, having bought up other edgy brand names such as Zoo York (for the skateboard crowd) and outerwear producer Avirex. The company also produces shoes, hats and watches, and high-end men's fashion "with just the right amount of swagger." There's even a streetwear magazine, Complex, dedicated to spreading Eckõ's "community of individuals" culture. Now a billion-dollar company, Eckõ has opened its own retail stores to stay in touch with its target market and test new ideas. For instance, controlling its own retail environment helped the company score a big win with (of all things) a high-end line of *Star Wars* shirts and hoodies. With your own stores, says Marc, you can "do more narrative-based things with the product."

Marc Ecko and his 50% partner, Seth Gerszberg, learned just in time that the "product" is not the brand. By focusing on finding a style and voice for urban youth, they turned the company into a champion of creativity and empowerment.

Today, that quest for authenticity (or "cred") continues. In 2007, Marc Ecko paid $752,467 for the baseball that controversial slugger Barry Bonds hit for his record-breaking 756th home run. He set up a website allowing customers to vote on whether he should donate the ball to the Baseball Hall of Fame in Cooperstown or shoot it into space. The winning idea: send it to the Hall with an asterisk cut into it to acknowledge the controversy over Bonds' use of steroids. Ecko's big stunt generated 10 million votes, millions of dollars' worth of free publicity—and cemented his rep as an outlaw with both authenticity and edge.

Turning opportunities into projects

Again, success is not just about identifying opportunities, but also ensuring that they get implemented. Each opportunity must become a project and each project needs a champion. Assign a project leader who is an "opportunity champion" for each project you plan to move forward. It will be their responsibility to work out the full extent of the opportunity and assess how and when it will get to market, and what resources will be required.

Implementing strategy

At this point, you have plotted your highest- and best-potential opportunities, created projects and assigned champions to each opportunity. They will refine implementation strategies that fit the overall strategy and develop a plan of action. Next, you need to take a look at developing the most relevant communications strategies and identifying your most effective tools.

Chapter

16

Step Six
Speaking to be heard

Good communications transform opportunity into results. Bad communications transform nothing.

Ken Tencer

Speaking effectively goes a long way to converting your opportunities into revenue and sustaining a relevant brand—as in having clear, compelling and consistent communications (strategies, messages and media). Too often, however, communication is the most overlooked component of a strategic plan.

If a tree falls in the forest and no one is there, does it make a sound?

The market is a huge, noisy forest. If you expect to survive, you must be there and you must be heard above the din. To do that, you must have something worth hearing. You must speak clearly enough to be heard, and be interesting enough so that people will listen. Tens of thousands of great products, services and ideas fail because no one notices them, or pays attention, or understands them or connects to them. No relationship.

The market is a huge, noisy forest. If you expect to survive, you must be there and you must be heard above the din. To do that, you must have something worth hearing.

Integrating the most effective communications tools allows you to not only carve out a unique position for your brand, but to constantly shape it for everchanging markets. If you listen to your customers at each step-to-market, they will tell you if your communications are working.

Matchmaking

All too often, people focus on speaking solely to the customer. But success comes from identifying all the people that you need to be speaking to—your communications touch-points: employees, salespeople, distributors, agents, stakeholders ... *and* customers. Only in this way can you create the most effective and efficient communication materials.

Essentially, you need to ensure that you know:

- What your most compelling story is
  (for your customers).
- Who you are speaking to.
- What you want to achieve with your communication
  (e.g., awareness, education, direct response,
  call to action).
- What action you want to induce
  (e.g., buy, trial, join, attend).
- How you are most effectively going to reach them
  (which media).

Now you can select the best communications tools based on who you are speaking to, what you want to say, and what you want your audience to do. This exercise ensures success by creating a context for the selection of communications vehicles rather than tolerating the all-too-common practice of going right to the perceived solution (e.g., "We need a website," or "we need a new brochure").

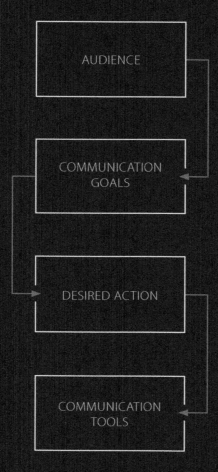

SELECTING
communication tools.

- Identify the supply chain that your product or service follows from inception to end-use (e.g., producer-agent-distributor-retailer-customer)
- Identify what is most important to communicate about your product or service to *each* group in the chain. Each part of the chain may have different needs (e.g., awareness, information, education, engagement), but you need to enforce consistency across all messages.
- Identify the different communications tools (e.g., advertising, websites, blogs, e-blast, videos, newsletters, tradeshows, sales presentations) in your tool set.
- Identify the best tools to reach and engage each group in the chain.

Common communications shortcomings

I have found that those companies who do not understand or do not value the power of a strong brand usually make many common mistakes. Here are a few:

- Inconsistency: Imagine a company that pins its brand on good customer service – and yet has an eight-layer touch-tone phone menu that frustrates consumers trying to get an answer or help. Then they have the gall to insert a voice message that says, "Your call is important to us" – and make you wait five more minutes.
- Misunderstanding of touch points: Making decisions based on a flawed understanding of effective communications by thinking, "It's only a fridge magnet, so we can let the printer design it." Except the fridge magnet is the one piece of communication that will live in the customer's home, on its most prominent

appliance, for the longest time. Why would you ever think of minimizing this inside-edge ambassador?

- Cutting the wrong corners: One client once tried to cut corners on its packaging, noting that "The label on the product doesn't have to be more than two colors because the bottle comes in a beautiful box." Oh and, when the box is opened and thrown away, what lives in the customer's home, representing your brand and reminding the customer of what to buy next time? The bottle, that's right – the one with the poorly conceived label.

- Not utilizing the power of digital and social and interactive media (i.e., Blogs, LinkedIn, Facebook, Pinterest, Buzzfeed, et al) to extend brand reach (and increasing these budgets) because they do not understand the "new" media. Or using new media without understanding the best ways to leverage its strengths.

- Not telling your brand story in the most persuasive, compelling and consistent way possible.

If history were taught in the form of stories, it would never be forgotten.

Rudyard Kipling (1865-1939)

Marketing is not a series of transactions between a company and its customers; it's all about building meaningful, ongoing relationships. The fundamentals of relationship marketing are based on each party not only understanding the tangible benefits they receive from each other, but about creating strong emotional bonds between the brand and its users. Building these relationships requires the very best in communications.

The full suite of marketing tools goes beyond traditional advertising or direct mail to create a complete spectrum of benefits:

1. Raise awareness and interest (the traditional function of advertising).
2. Provide information and context (long-copy print and web functionality).
3. Induce action (direct response – direct mail, online, interactive).
4. Promote engagement (web functionality).
5. Establish brand advocacy (public relations, web and social media).

This list oversimplifies the intent and the results of each communications tool - after all, they are very complex, and you can achieve many cross-platform benefits by integrating different media and strategies. For example, good advertising can promote engagement and move product, just as social media can raise awareness, create word-of-mouth and sell.

Implementation

Implementation is all about turning marketing into a powerful force. The most effective and efficient way to do this is to understand who you are speaking to, what is important to them, and how you want them to respond – before establishing your communications mix.

Chapter **17**

Success Comes From Action:
The Never-ending Step

*Plans and opportunities without sustainable and
measurable action are like a canoe without a
Paddle—leaving you you-know-where.*

Ken Tencer

The *90% Rule* takes you beyond the mythical – sometimes futile – dependency on annual corporate retreats, sporadic seminars and consultancy quick-fixes because its role is to solve your ongoing needs (i.e., more innovation, better opportunities, stronger brand, more sustainable growth). The *90% Rule* gives you a concrete, built-in process anchored to measurable and actionable opportunities that allow you *to get the most out of what you already have.* It puts innovation on the front burner, every day.

*Whenever anything is being accomplished,
it is being done, I have learned,
by a monomaniac with a mission.*

Peter Drucker

Action-Innovation-Plan (AIP)

If the action is to be consistent, then the process must be integrated into your operations so that the opportunities and priorities are continually front-and-center for everybody to see, revisit and recalibrate. Nothing is more unpredictable than the marketplace, and nothing is more elusive than trying to keep up with the market. It is essential that you provide everyone in your organization with a means to stay on top of what is needed. And innovate, innovate, innovate.

Consider this Action-Innovation-Plan as a model for embracing innovation and constantly recalibrating to meet changing needs.

1) Business Development Meetings (weekly or monthly): Transform your regular sales and marketing meetings to include innovation. The first step is to have each project leader (opportunity champion) present status reports and solicit input from the group. This helps you to keep track of ideas and live projects, and engages your team through ongoing involvement, letting them know that their efforts are being implemented.

2) The second step is to task all team members to bring in new ideas — things that they see happening within your marketplace and from other, unrelated industries. Encourage everyone to attend business conferences, seminars, workshops, and peer groups, and to listen more closely (and more often) to customers in order to increase idea flow and generation. This second step keeps the whole team focused on opportunities, everyday.

3) Innovation Breakouts (quarterly): These are collaborative sessions to review markets and products, exchange ideas, share new thinking and determine how to drive ongoing innovation. From these discussions you update and revise the action plan as required.

Task all team members to bring in new ideas – things that they see happening within your marketplace and from other, unrelated industries. Encourage everyone to attend business conferences, seminars, workshops, and peer groups, and to listen more closely (and more often) to customers in order to increase idea flow and generation.

4) Customer Summit (annually): Remember, nobody is more important than your customers. New ideas help to keep them engaged with your company. Take the time to ask them what challenges they are having or anticipate having, and how your company can step up to help to solve them. These are formal discussions with your customers – best conducted by a third party – to gather feedback and discuss their needs, market trends, industry issues and shared opportunities. These discussions nearly always require you to revise your ongoing action plan – and that's a good thing. In business-to-consumer organizations, encourage open innovation through electronic media. This can help you garner feedback and ideas daily.

5) Annual Summit (on-site or off): This is a comprehensive evaluation of progress, problems and emerging opportunities. It is also the time to review strategies and resources, and recalibrate programs. From these discussions you make revisions to strategies – if any – and readjust your tactics accordingly. It's a periodic review and refinement of your ongoing process.

These five action steps will help you integrate disciplined, systematic creativity throughout your organization so that it fuels continuous action, creates widespread innovation and drives sustainable growth.

Remember, nobody is more important than your customers. New ideas help to keep them engaged with your company. Take the time to ask them what challenges they are having or anticipate having, and how your company can step up to help to solve them.

Part
Four

The next 10%

There is nothing more rewarding than working in a dynamic, forward-thinking organization – for your psyche and your wallet!

Chapter

18

The Best of Both Worlds

"And" not "or."

Ken Tencer

Strategy is essential, but it is the thinking that creates strategies that sits at the core of how a business shapes its future. Time and again, I meet with experienced, senior management who talk in terms of strategy being something that is calculated from data alone. Not true. Great strategies are fashioned from creative thinking, not simply deduced through logical thinking.

In his book *A Whole New Mind,* author Daniel Pink states, "The future belongs to a different kind of person with a different kind of mind ... creative and emphatic 'right-brain' thinkers whose abilities mark the fault line between who gets ahead and who doesn't."[14] I do agree with Pink's idea that success will spring from a "different kind of person". But I also believe that most of us are already, at our core, that kind of "different", creative person just waiting to be (re) discovered. As thought-leaders like Edward De Bono[15] and Howard Gardner of Harvard[16] say, we are all – well, most of us – capable of creative thinking.

---

[14] *A Whole New Mind, Daniel H. Pink, Riverhead Books/Penguin, 2005*
[15] Six Thinking Hats by Edward De Bono
[16] *Leading Minds by Howard Gardner*

Roger Martin, long-time dean of the Rotman School of Management at the University of Toronto, makes the point: "In a generative thinking process all strategic-thinking activities are oriented towards creating instead of calculating – inventing instead of finding ... Strategists must leave the intellectual safety of generally accepted concepts to explore new ideas guided by little else than their intuition."[17]

This and that: Two little words and a world of difference

I happened to be reading Roger Martin's 2007 book, *The Opposable Mind*, at the same time that I was delivering a *90% Rule* seminar. During the seminar, we delved into a discussion about the potential services that the company could offer to its customer base. Sales was pushing for the longest list of services possible but finance wanted to offer only the most profitable ones. One participant said, "We can't do both, we have to choose between 'this' or 'that', comprehensive services or high margins". Actually, they didn't have to choose. By bundling services together, we achieved customer-centric services packages that were both easy to sell and achieved acceptable profit margins. Win-win. That got me thinking about Martin's discussion about the pitfalls of "either-or" decision-making.

The best of both worlds

As an entrepreneur, I am always pushing for more. I am pressing for the creation of something different and engaging to inspire and capture a whole new group of customers. The notion of "this" **or** "that" doesn't exist for me because it represents unnecessary compromise. Or, more to the point, the easy way out. As an entrepreneur, I always push for "this" **and** "that." Because **and** represents more ... for the customer and ultimately for my business.

[17] *The Opposable Mind, Roger Martin, Harvard Business School Press, 2007*

The notion of "this" *or* "that" doesn't exist for me because it represents unnecessary compromise. Or, more to the point, the easy way out. As an entrepreneur, I always push for "this" *and* "that." Because *and* represents more ... for the customer and ultimately for my business.

I push teams to find a way to combine and execute ideas, to merge them into one whole new idea, a breakthrough innovation. It all begins by changing one simple word but what a difference a word can make. Thinking in terms of "and" rather than "or" can be mindset and game-changing. It is at the heart of innovative thinking.

The challenge for innovators is to develop a pragmatic means of demonstrating, to a wide range of people (not just CEOs and senior management), how to approach "this *and* that" thinking. The solution lies in something that I have been using for years, the Venn diagram.

Let's call one circle of the Venn diagram "this" and the other one "that." I want to identify the point at which the circles intersect, because this point represents convergence, value, growth and opportunity. These intersecting circles help people to visualize how two seemingly opposing ideas or different directions once separated by the word "or" can come together, find common ground and become a whole new idea built on the word "and". We call this the best of both worlds.

Most importantly, at this point of intersection we also achieve the maximum value to the customer -- because by focusing on this point of intersection, we have chosen to add value, not to compromise it. It is a simple realization and a straight-forward exercise that can prove galvanizing.

There are many examples of how seemingly opposing ideas have come together in an incredible new concept:

✔ Target stores have brought together competitive pricing **and** fashion-forward design in their now famous 'masstige' platform.

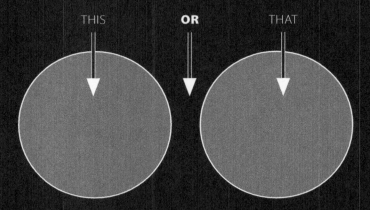

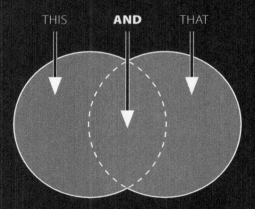

THIS and THAT
diagram.

✔ Apologies to the lover of the old box-frame design but, after years of trying, Volvo has brought together its platform of industry-leading safety **and** an aesthetically pleasing design.

✔ Bose Wave® Music System has melded incredible sound quality, affordability **and** an incredibly small stature.

Admittedly, it's not easy to get people to embrace this concept. Not everyone is comfortable with giving up "this" to get to "that." Even when they do, it doesn't happen over night. James Dyson created 5,127 prototypes of his first vacuum cleaner before being satisfied.

Whether it's attributes such as price versus quality, or functions like sales versus marketing, try applying the Venn diagram next time you are struggling to bring collective new thinking to the table. It's a powerful visual tool that presents the powerful end goal of mutual opportunity – company and customer –– for all stakeholders to see.

The melding of ideas to create opportunities is a big part of the *90% Rule* process. It's how the future begins to take shape. Because it's where once parallel streams of linear thinking creatively merge into significant, actionable and game-changing opportunity.

Let's call one circle of the Venn diagram "this" and the other one "that." I want to identify the point at which the circles intersect, because this point represents convergence, value, growth and opportunity.

Chapter 19

Making a Decision

Make decisions grounded in intellect, instinct and process. It beats the old process, of throwing darts blindfolded.

Ken Tencer

Here's a quick question to ask yourself before you jump into something – a gut check that I use often: "Is it yummy or is it yucky?" Let me explain.

As a young entrepreneur, I was stalled in trying to make a business decision relating to the growth of my business. At dinner one night with a successful, self-made businessman, I asked his advice. I was expecting some elevated insight that would sound wise and worldly. That's not what I got, but nonetheless it has stuck with me for years. He picked up the sugar bowl in one hand and the saltshaker in the other saying, "I want you to make a gut decision." Then he asked, "Which opportunity is yummy, which is yucky?"

I wish that every decision were truly that simple. However, when you use a systematic process that relates tactical decisions to visionary thinking, then what might appear to be a gut decision or a hunch is actually firmly grounded in what you already know -- the vision, mission, goals, objectives and criteria that you have developed with your team.

At Spyder Works we call it an "Intellectual Gut Check.™" This is when you connect what you intellectually understand (i.e., you know that despite looking similar, salt and sugar are different) with an instinctive gut feeling that you have developed over time. You choose the sugar over the salt based on bringing together previous process-driven information and the emotional feeling of the question/decision in front of you: How does it *feel,* yummy or yucky? The decision to pursue an opportunity becomes more clear.

I find some of the most brilliant breakthroughs are the simplest ones, insights that most people miss. It's not because we're not smart enough; we just tend to see only the complexity in those things that we are too close to. We don't pull back and view the complexity from a higher level, from a different perspective. We don't see the difference between sugar and salt, between nickels and dimes.

The *90% Rule* is grounded in this principle of developing an ingrained process and set of criteria, and building a cumulative and collective body of thought that minimizes guesswork throughout the organization. The process eliminates unfounded gut decisions by linking them to knowledge, thereby encouraging and supporting well-founded 'gut' decisions. All the thinking, questioning, prodding and researching now come together, leveraging the instinct and intellect of many different people working closely as entrepreneurial partners. This is where innovation springs from – every day!

Pass the sugar, please.

I find some of the most brilliant breakthroughs are the simplest ones, insights that most people miss. It's not because we're not smart enough; we just tend to see only the complexity in those things that we are too close to.

Chapter 20

Growing Your Own

Watch a person's feet, not their mouth.

John Paulo Cardoso

One of my favorite advertisements was an early one for the American Express Gold Card. The headline ran: "Nobody ever promised you a rose garden, so you grew your own." That attitude resonated with me as a young business student and aspiring entrepreneur, and has since stuck with me for decades. It is a constant reminder for me of the principle that life makes no promises, but it offers plenty of opportunities. In fact, the process set out in this book grew out of my continuing search for better and better ways to uncover more and more of the opportunities that life presents.

I hope that it has already caused you to examine, question, change and apply new approaches to the way you think about your business. I hope that it will help you take on the day with a dose of audacity, disrupt the status quo, and cause disturbances in your marketplace. I hope it helps you become more innovative, in product and in process. And I hope you begin now to see how the leverage power of the *90% Rule* can make you, your team and your business breakthrough innovators.

As always, I like to end where I began. Remember the four fundamentals that underlie everything that we have worked through. They demonstrate how easily you can transform your business.

1) The 90% Rule helps you foster continuous innovation and growth through the doctrine of entrepreneurial thinking – "innovation against all odds" – by leveraging intellectual and customer capital, continually generating ideas and opportunities, and executing it all without bundles of additional money.

2) You need a disciplined process that builds on "the best" in your organization, your people, your products and your services. Using the principles of entrepreneurial thinking, this process elevates innovation to new levels

3) The challenge is to install and implement a systematic and iterative process that pursues opportunities that you are already 90% capable of achieving.

4) It's easier than you think.

The opportunity is yours. It is both a small step *and* a giant leap. Just take it!

Chapter **21**

Unpack Your Bags and Stay A While: Applying Innovation to A More Fulfilled You

The 90% Rule is not a formula; it's a philosophy.

Ken Tencer

In life, as in business, The 90% Rule can be a great enabler. The principle is that if you truly understand what your business is already best at, then 90% of the innovation you need for new growth is already waiting to be released. The 90% Rule is designed to help business leaders keep their companies dynamic and fresh, and create stronger and better growth.

Just ask yourself what minor tweaks and adaptations might launch you into adjacent markets, and you'll be off and running. It's that simple. This 10% additional effort can take your business into a new era of continual, low-risk growth. When it becomes part of your regular business routine, the 90% Rule will create a forward-looking culture that is constantly innovating and finding new ways to both serve customers and engage employees. You probably won't be surprised to learn that many employees, after reading this book, discovered something else: personal growth.

Life principles

People found that the 90% Rule also applies to their careers and daily lives. In retrospect, this makes sense. Just as in business, we can all get caught up in front-burner issues and mundane routines in our personal lives. In doing so, we often lose sight of some of the essential ingredients that make up our core self: Who we are; What we're good at; What we're not good at; What we really want; and how to accomplish the things that are important *to us*. Instead of focusing on our interests and strengths, we fall into a rut. In business and in life, ruts are repetitive sinkholes that consume energy and time; they are not profitable places to be stuck in.

In business, the 90% Rule encourages owners and managers to shed their sacred cows, the old habits they thought indispensible, the anchors that dictate business as usual. Obviously, it's essential to question sacred cows in businesses and in our personal lives. Oddly enough, the more sacred we believe something to be, the more dispensable it often turns out to be.

In life, we all collect baggage – ideas, perceptions, cultural norms and social understandings – about who we are and what we can and cannot do. Much of what we lug around in those bags has been imposed on us by others (family, friends, teachers, and so on), and no longer reflects who we really are. But regardless of who imposed what, it has been our decision to carry that baggage around with us. What many people have discovered is that the principles of The 90% Rule helped them take the time to review their own personal "baggage" and make decisions about what is really important, and which sacred cows can be put out to pasture. For the individual, it lightens the load, and makes their journey easier and more satisfying. Unpack those bags. Ironically, this is also a great example of the simple-adaptive innovation we talked about early in this book: Same product, new application.

Not being an expert in the psychological aspect of such issues, I asked a long-time friend, clinical psychologist Ian Shulman, for his thoughts. He endorsed the importance of reflection and questioning in our daily lives, and agreed that this is a cathartic process that everyone should go through – one very much like the 90% Rule. "It's important to recognize the invisible but influential biases we live with," says Dr. Shulman. "Always present, these 'mental lenses' tell us how to interpret events that happen in our daily lives and inform the decisions we make next." He added a few examples of the sort of questions that can lead to profitable breakthroughs: "Am I a good and worthwhile person who also happened to get a speeding ticket, or did I get the ticket because I am careless? Do I have what it takes to attempt this difficult assignment, or do I just know that I can't do it?"

Dr. Shulman says decisions such as these "happen automatically, based on instantaneous tallies of life experiences. Even though the answers might seem crystal-clear and feel undeniably true, they are nothing more than mental events that exist within the mind. Of greater importance is what one chooses to do in that next moment." How we see things directly affects our judgment and what we do far more than we realize.

Dr. Shulman's observations can also be equated to the lens through which we see our businesses – filled with old thoughts, sacred cows and accepted behavior. It's why the status quo is so difficult to change. Yet, if we can start by simply looking at the next 10% – "What might be" – the view through that lens becomes quite different. So too in our personal lives.

Once we reflect on and redefine what is important to us personally (i.e., our history, core values, strengths, weaknesses, what is, what can be), we can identify the next 10% and the steps that will help us move closer to becoming the best people we can be. This is rewarding. It's a simple process of revaluation and redefining that can lead to considerable renewal. And it can stay with us, guiding us, and ensuring we don't get off track again.

Dr. Shulman says, "Begin to appreciate that we can decide who we want to be, and then start taking steps to create that way of living." In other words, personal change and improvement – so difficult for so many – is possible. It's all part of a process of re-examining and reimagining.

One more salient point from Dr. Shulman: For best results, we need to make sure the people we welcome into our life also have their baggage in order. Hopefully it's not all oversized and crammed with clutter. Their baggage should fit comfortably next to ours in the luggage compartment. "Find people and activities that are consistent with your more conscious decisions," says Dr. Shulman. "This will keep you in better tune with the rhythm of your life and prepare you to stretch and grow in the right directions."

Starting now, I hope that you will unleash your audacity, exorcise your sacred cows and lighten your baggage (both business and personal), and take steps toward liberating the insight, inspiration and imagination that can make you a true innovator. The good news: It's easier than you think.

And you are already 90% of the way there.

After
Word

About the authors
Acknowledgements

KEN TENCER is a branding and innovation thought leader who helps organizations master better futures. He is co-developer of The 90% Rule, a success-tested innovation process that enables businesses of all sizes to identify new market and strategic opportunities, and map out relevant, high-potential growth opportunities.

Ken is a successful entrepreneur and business developer who has built international-scale companies spanning manufacturing, product development, distribution and professional services. As CEO of Spyder Works, he helps companies with both branding and innovation strategy.

Ken holds a Bachelor of Commerce with Honors from the Sprott School of Business, Carleton University in Ottawa, Canada and earned a Masters of Science in International Management from Boston University while studying at their campus in Brussels, Belgium. Ken has also received a joint certificate from the Institute of Corporate Directors and the Joseph L. Rotman School of Management, University of Toronto, for the small and medium-sized enterprises board effectiveness program. He has sat on a number of for and not-for-profit Boards, and has served as a member of the Advisory Board for the Conference Board of Canada's Centre for Business Innovation.

JOHN PAULO CARDOSO is Chief Creative Officer of Spyder Works Inc. and a world-class creative director who believes that true design brings meaning to the mass of unrelated needs, wants, ideas and perceptions. John says, "Design thinking is at the core of making sense of everything, from the complexity of overabundance to the simplicity of oneness."

John is responsible for ensuring that creativity, in all its forms, through all the firm's work, manifests itself in business results. As John says, "Creativity represents the emotional elements of every experience, but if it does not move the business, what's the point of the experience."

With over twenty years in design, John has brought his unconventional thinking to clients in many industries, from emerging businesses to multinational corporations.

John founded Spyder Desktop Studio in 1992 to support the development of leading international brands such as Agfa, Estée Lauder and Revlon. In 2003, he formed Spyder Works Inc. with Ken, transforming the firm from a leading provider of creative design to a comprehensive provider of business and marketing strategy, integrated design and communications.

At Spyder Works John leads the creative team with the innovative branding model Eight Steps to Brand Re(Invention)™. John is also the co-developer of the firm's model for integrated business and design thinking, Building Business by Design®.

John has an Honors BA in Fine Art History from the University of Toronto and holds a certificate of design from the internationally acclaimed Art Centre in Toronto.

Acknowledgements

When I founded a company called Spyder in 1992, it was with the intent of briefly supporting my wife Elizabeth and me while I finished my second undergraduate degree at the University of Toronto. Quickly, the business started to grow organically as I worked closely with Estée Lauder in Canada and New York. This organic growth led me to a small boardroom attached to a manufacturing plant run by this guy who was throwing around the idea of a product called "Totally Fried Hair". Little did I know that Ken Tencer would become my business partner as we transformed Spyder into Spyder Works and that he would become CEO of the company as we built on the foundation of creative and pragmatic thinking – which would allow us to "think + do".

Through the business building process we came to understand who we were, what we stood for and how to define our core values. We were, and still are, convinced of the benefits of combining creative and pragmatic thinking into an integrated process. We have always believed that we could find a "better way" and were influenced by our favorite anecdote from the early space program—how the Americans spent millions of dollars developing a pen that would work in space while the Russians simply used a pencil.

When creativity and logic are fused, you get innovation—and simplicity. We wanted to build a company and a philosophy that would demystify and simplify the integration of business strategy and design thinking, then give other companies a pragmatic and systematic means of actually achieving it. This book is an acknowledgement of having reached an important milestone on that journey. *Cause a Disturbance* is the culmination of many years of pragmatic hands-on research, practical experience and the innate inspiration we both acquired growing up in entrepreneurial families.

Through the process, Ken and I have become indebted to friends, colleagues and others who have shepherded this project through to completion. We will try to acknowledge them here. Just as it takes a village to raise a child, it takes a group of people to nurture, shape and write a book. From its conception to the final manuscript, we are grateful to all who have supported and helped us along the way.

We thank professor Nicolas Papadopoulos who encouraged and explained to Ken that, while a book must center around a focused idea, the sum of words is comparable to the number of e-mails and reports that he wrote in a short span of time. This inspired Ken to begin our first book *The 90% Rule*—to lock himself in a hotel room for a long weekend to write the first ten thousand words. From there the momentum just kept on going and *Cause a Disturbance* came to life.

A thank you to Rick Spence and Norm Oulster who pushed us to keep going and write a second book about our thinking and process who recognized and supported our somewhat different and "refreshing" approach to business, and to our publicist Tom Martin, who has supported our vision and encouraged us to take the time to make things right. As well, our trusted advisors, who have been a guide and sounding-board: Marion Plunkett, Philip Mendes da Costa, Roy Sieben, Adrian Davis, Katherine Van de Mark and Elaine Holding. Last but not least, we would like to thank David Hughes. Without his encouragement, advice, perseverance, insight and special talent this book would not have come to fruition. Thank you David.

To our friends, extended families and colleagues, who supported and inspired us in various ways that they only know how and we will be always in their debt: Allan Lever, Leslie Hayman, Lori Freeman, Eric Klein, Randy Remme, Diana Hancock, Tony and Tammy Cardoso, Chris and Kim Tardif, Dan and Maureen Pharand, Carlo and Michelle Chiazza, Sandra and Joe Cardoso, Mark and Steph Tardif, Kimberly and Frank Ranieri, João Monteiro, José Pinto Cardoso, Warren Blatt, Carolyn Shaw, Gaston and Corinne (Corky) Tardif.

Also, we thank others who played an essential role in continuing to frame our work around projects that offered an exploration into our process—all our clients who never stop inspiring us to great heights and gave us crucial feedback: Beverly Topping, Margaret Parent, Marlene Novack, Sue Paish, Wayne Parent, Fred Stewart, Vicki Jordan, Yahya Abbas, Ian Hancock, Allan Farber, Gary Lifman, Allan Nackan, Andre Mazerolle, Mark Liberman, Lance Alexander, Sherry Abbott, Lori Baggett, Tibor Choleva, Sonia Doan, Laurie Dowley, Greg van den Hoogen and Pat Diamond.

A final thank you to those who are closest and dearest to us, our families. Without the support of our amazing families none of this would be possible. A special thank you to Esther, Laura, Tommy and Sofia. Thank you to Elizabeth Cardoso who manages all the important details of my life and keeping us on track with our three very busy boys Noah, Nathaniel and Quinn. Lastly, we thank our parents David Tencer, Glenys Tencer, Manuel Pinto Cardoso, and Concieção Cardoso.

Ken Tencer and John Paulo Cardoso

CPSIA information can be obtained at www.ICGtesting.com
Printed in the USA
BVOW11s0244090414

349597BV00005BA/7/P

31192020643860